MAC OS X TIGER

NICK VANDOME

in easy steps

In easy steps is an imprint of Computer Step
Southfield Road · Southam
Warwickshire CV47 0FB · United Kingdom
www.ineasysteps.com

Notice of Liability

Every effort has been made to ensure that this book contains accurate and
current information. However, Computer Step and the author shall not be
liable for any loss or damage suffered by readers as a result of any information
contained herein.

Trademarks

Mac OS X® is a registered trademark of Apple Computer, Inc. All other
trademarks are acknowledged as belonging to their respective companies.

Printed and bound in the United Kingdom

ISBN 1-84078-294-3

Table of Contents

Introducing OS X Tiger

OS X Tiger is the latest operating system from Apple Computers. It is promoted as being easy and enjoyable to use and also incredibly stable for a computer operating system. This chapter introduces OS X, shows you how to install it and also some of its fundamental features.

Covers

Chapter One

About OS X

Apple Computers have always been known for their ease of use and OS X Tiger takes this to a new level. In addition, it also makes it a lot easier for users to share files between Macs and Windows based PCs. This has been a problem in the past and with OS X the barriers between the two sets of computer users have been broken down to a certain degree.

In 1984 Apple Computers introduced a new operating system (OS) for its Macintosh computers and, at the time, it was revolutionary. Instead of having to access programs and files through lines of lengthy computer code commands, users could navigate their way through Apple computers using a new Graphical User Interface (GUI). This produced the same results as the previous method, but it was much easier for the user: instead of having to type in lines of computer coding it was possible to access files and programs by clicking on buttons, icons and drop down menus. This ease of use was a major factor in the mass adoption of personal computers and this type of operating system soon began to appear on all personal computers, not just Macs.

Over the years Apple refined its OS and added more and more functions with each new release. However, like any operating system the Mac OS was not without its problems: it was as prone to crashes as any other operating system and it had its own quirky idiosyncrasies, such as extension conflicts (when two programs refused to cohabit on the same machine).

When Apple decided to upgrade their OS from version 9 they were faced with two choices: add more code to what was becoming an incredibly complicated structure for the Apple programmers to work with, or, create an entirely new program from scratch. Thankfully, they chose the second option, and the result is OS X.

UNIX is an operating system that has traditionally been used for large commercial mainframe computers. It is renowned for its stability and ability to be used within different computing environments.

In some ways OS X is a contradiction of Apple's original philosophy: while it retains and enhances its traditional ease of use, it is also based on the UNIX programming language, the very type of thing that Apple was trying to get away from in 1984. The reason it is based on UNIX is that this is a very stable operating environment and ensures that OS X is one of the most stable consumer operating systems that has ever been designed. However, for most users, they can be blissfully unaware of the very existence of UNIX if they want and just enjoy its benefits while using the new Aqua interface of OS X and all of the advantages that this brings. For the programming expert, there is also an option of delving into UNIX itself and getting to grips with this side of the program. Tiger is the fourth version of OS X and one of the most advanced operating system seen to date.

Installing OS X

The first step to install OS X is to insert the CD-ROM into the CD drive. The disk should run automatically and the installation can then proceed as follows:

Double-click here to read any last-minute release notes

Make sure you read any of the online documentation before you install OS X. These documents, which are usually in PDF format, can contain useful general information and also any late news about the program that was released after it was produced.

2 Double-click on the Install Mac OS X icon to begin the installation process

3 Enter a name and password

The name and password that is entered at the beginning of the installation process will be needed if you want to set up your computer for multiple users. For more details on this, see Chapter Eight. In some cases, a password is also required for installing software updates.

Authenticate

Install Mac OS X requires that you type your password.

Name: Nick Vandome

Password: ••••••••

▶ Details

(?)

(Cancel) (OK)

4 Click OK

Install Mac OS X

Mac OS X Tiger

Click the button below to restart your computer and begin the installation process.

(Restart)

The registration process consists of entering a few details and then moving through a series of dialog windows. In most cases all you have to do is accept the default settings and options that are displayed.

5 Click Restart. Your computer will then shut down and start up again and take you through the rest of the registration process

The OS X environment

The first most noticeable element about OS X is its elegant user interface. This has been designed to create a user friendly graphic overlay to the UNIX operating system at the heart of OS X and it is a combination of rich colors and sharp, original graphics. The main elements that make up the initial OS X environment are:

The Apple menu is standardized throughout OS X, regardless of the program in use.

Apple menu   Menu bar   Windows   Disk icons

The disk icons sit on the desktop and identify which disks are connected to the computer. This includes the Mac hard drive and any external devices that are connected, such as a Zip drive or a CD/DVD drive.

The Dock   Desktop

The Dock is designed to help make organizing and opening items as quick and easy as possible. For a detailed look at the Dock, see Chapter Two.

Aqua interface

The name given by Apple to its OS X interface is Aqua. This describes the graphical appearance of the operating system. Essentially, it is just the cosmetic appearance of the elements within the operating system, but they combine to give OS X a rich visual look and feel. Some of the main elements of the Aqua interface are:

The graphics used in OS X are designed in a style known as Quartz.

Menus

Menus in OS X contain commands for the operating system and any relevant programs. If there is an arrow next to a command it means there are subsequent options for the item:

If OS X has no preferred option in a dialog box, all of the option buttons are gray. However, it is still possible to click on the button of your choice.

Window buttons

These appear in any open OS X window and can be used to manipulate the window.

The red window button is used to close a window; the amber one to minimize it and the green one to expand it.

Option buttons

Whenever a dialog box with separate options is accessed, OS X highlights the suggested option with a pulsing blue button. This can be accepted by clicking on it or by pressing Enter. If you do not want to accept this option, click on another button in the dialog box.

Running OS 9 and OS X

Even though OS X is up to version 4 (10.4), there are still a lot of users operating programs that were written before the appearance of OS X. Apple overcomes this by bundling the previous operating system, OS 9, with OS X. OS 9 is automatically installed along with OS X. This means that there are in effect two operating systems on the same computer. For newer programs OS X will automatically be used to open and run them, but for older ones, OS 9 will open up and run the programs. This is known as opening programs in Classic mode. This happens automatically when you open a program that is not able to run on OS X: the OS 9 environment will open and run the program.

If you previously ran OS 9 on your computer it is possible to see the contents of your old desktop by double-clicking on the Applications (Mac OS 9) folder, located on your hard drive. The contents of the OS 9 desktop are then available, exactly as they were before OS X was installed:

Programs that were written for OS 9 and have not been updated at all are known as Classic programs. Programs written for OS 9 but amended so that they can be opened by OS X are known as Carbon programs. Programs written specifically for OS X are known as Cocoa programs.

Classic mode

If programs are not compatible with OS X they will open in Classic mode, i.e. with OS 9. This happens automatically and it is not always possible to know in which mode a program will open until you access it. In general, programs that were previously used in OS 9, and have not been upgraded, will open in Classic mode. To open a program in Classic mode:

Even if programs open in Classic mode, their icons can still be placed on the OS X Dock. For more details on the Dock, see Chapter Two.

1 Open a program from the OS 9 folder or the Dock

Dreamweaver 4 alias

2 Classic mode is activated to open the program. This takes a few seconds

Classic is starting

Stop

▶ Show Mac OS 9 startup window

Any programs that you had under a previous Mac operating system should run in Classic mode on a computer using OS X.

3 The program opens in Classic mode, i.e. with OS 9, and it can then be used in the same way as any other program, except that it does not have the OS X user interface

	File	Edit	View	Insert	M
New				⌘N	
New from Template...					
Open...				⌘O	
Open in Frame...				⇧⌘O	
Close				⌘W	
Save				⌘S	
Save As...				⇧⌘S	
Save as Template...					

Background on UNIX

UNIX is the powerful and robust operating system that is the foundation on which OS X runs. In fact, OS X is essentially a very impressive graphical interface placed on top of a version of UNIX known as Darwin.

UNIX was developed in the early 1970s by programmers who wanted to design an operating system that could run on any platform, i.e. different types of computers. Up until then, each operating system had generally been designed for a specific type of computer. Another benefit of UNIX was that it was designed to be available to the whole development community. The program that was used to create UNIX is the now widely used C language.

In addition to OS X on consumer computers Apple have also released a server that runs on UNIX. This is called XServer and it is used to run and manage computer networks.

UNIX first gained popularity in academic institutions and it was then taken on by government organizations. Its adoption by Apple as the foundation for OS X has seen UNIX move into the mainstream of consumer computing. UNIX's greatest strength is its stability, while its greatest weakness is perhaps its non-user-friendliness. Apple have made the most of the former and overcome the latter with its Aqua interface and Quartz graphics.

For people with experience of UNIX, programming can be performed within OS X in the Terminal window. This is the gateway into the UNIX environment and it can be located in Applications>Utilities from the Finder. If you are not familiar with UNIX, you need never worry about it or the Terminal again.

Working with UNIX in the Terminal is not for the uninitiated, or the faint-hearted

Security for OS X

Security is a major issue for all computer users. This includes concerns about the unauthorized physical access of information on a computer (i.e. an individual viewing and changing files on a computer) to virtual attacks on a system from viruses or spyware. OS X has functions for decreasing the chances of these types of problems. These include options for setting master passwords, using the OS X firewall and creating keychain passwords.

For more information about accessing and using System Preferences see

Chapter Two.

FileVault

This is located within the Security preferences of the System Preferences and it can be used to protect access to your computer:

1 Click here to set a master password. This is another password, in addition to the one that can be set at login, that can be used to lock the contents of your home folder

If you set a master password for your home folder and then forget your login password you will not be able to access your home folder.

2 Click here to turn on the FileVault

3 Click here to set preferences for how the computer is accessed if it has gone to sleep

Firewall

The OS X firewall can be used to block malicious or unwanted viruses or spyware from entering your computer if it is connected to the Internet or a network. To access the firewall:

1 Access the Sharing preferences of the System Preferences

2 Click here to activate the firewall

3 Check these boxes on to specify areas that are exempt from the firewall

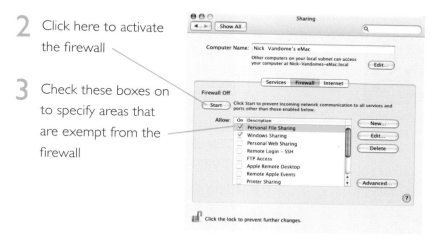

Keychain

The keychain facility is one that can be used to store different passwords for items such as applications, servers and websites. When you open one of these items, the keychain provides the password so that you do not have to remember numerous different passwords. Keychain Access is located within the Utilities folder.

When you first login to your Mac user account (usually when you first set up your Mac computer) your login password becomes your initial keychain.

New keychains can be created by opening the Keychain Access utility and selecting File>New Keychain from the Menu bar. You can then enter a name and password for each new keychain. Keychains can be very effective when used on networks that are used by multiple users.

Shutting down

The Apple menu (which can be accessed by clicking on the Apple icon at the top left corner of the desktop or any subsequent OS X window) has been standardized in OS X. This means that it has the same options regardless of the program in which you are working. This has a number of advantages, not least is the fact that it makes it easier to shut down your Mac. When shutting down, there are three options that can be selected:

If you install new software you will usually have to restart your computer before it takes effect.

- Sleep. This puts the Mac into hibernation mode, i.e. the screen goes blank and the hard drive becomes inactive. This state is maintained until the mouse is moved or a key is pressed on the keyboard. This then wakes up the Mac and it is ready to continue work

- Restart. This closes down the Mac and then restarts it again. This can be useful if you have added new software and your computer requires a restart to make it active

- Shut Down. This closes down the Mac completely once you have finished working

When shutting down, make sure you have saved all of your open documents, although OS X will prompt you to do this if you have forgotten.

Click here to access the Apple menu

Click here to access one of the shut down options

Up and running with OS X

This chapter looks at some of the features of OS X that can help you get up and running quickly with the operating system. These include the Dock for organizing and accessing all of the elements of the computer, the system preferences for the way the computer looks and operates, working with items on the desktop and functions for organizing individual programs.

Covers

Chapter Two

Introducing the Dock

The Dock is one of the main innovative elements of OS X. Its main function is to help organize and access programs, folders and files. In addition, with its rich translucent colors and elegant graphical icons, it also makes an aesthetically pleasing addition to the desktop. The main things to remember about the Dock are:

- It is divided into two: programs go on the left of the dividing line; all other items go on the right

- It can be edited in just about any way you choose

By default the Dock appears at the bottom of the screen

The Dock is always displayed as a line of icons, but this can be orientated either vertically or horizontally.

Items on the Dock can be opened by clicking on them once, rather than having to double-click on them.

Programs go here   Dividing line   All other open items go here

Setting Dock preferences

As with most elements of OS X, the Dock can be modified in numerous ways. This can affect both the appearance of the Dock and the way it operates. To set Dock preferences:

Select Apple Menu>Dock from the menu bar

The Apple menu is constantly available in OS X, regardless of the program in which you are working. The menu options are also constant in all applications.

You will not be able to make the Dock size too large so that some of the icons would not be visible on the desktop. By default, the Dock is resized so that everything is always visible.

2 Select the general preferences here

3 Click here to access more Dock preferences (below)

The Dock Preferences allow you to change its size, orientation, the way icons appear and effects for when items are minimized:

The "Position on screen" options enable you to place the Dock on the left, right or bottom of the screen

The Dock always sits on top of any open windows. You may therefore want to move its position if it obscures part of an open window. This can sometimes be an issue if the Dock is positioned at the bottom of the screen.

The Dock cannot be moved by dragging it, this can only be done in the Dock Preferences window.

Drag the Dock Size slider to increase or decrease the size of the Dock

Check on the Magnification box and drag the slider to determine the size to which icons are enlarged when the cursor is moved over them

When the cursor is moved over an item in the Dock, the name of that item is displayed above it.

The effects that are applied to items when they are minimized is one of the features of OS X (it is not absolutely necessary but it sums up the Apple ethos of trying to enhance the user experience as much as possible).

The Genie effect shrinks the item to be minimized like a genie going back into its lamp

The other animated effect for minimizing open windows is the Scale effect, where the window scales itself down proportionately to fit on the Dock.

Open windows can also be minimized by double-clicking on their title bar (the thinly lined bar at the top of the window, next to the three window buttons.)

Manual resizing

In addition to changing the size of the Dock by using the Dock Preference dialog box, it can also be resized manually:

Drag vertically on the Dock dividing line to increase or decrease its size

Accessing items

The Dock can be used to access everything within your Mac computer. In most cases it will be the starting point before you start any new operation or project. It can be used to open programs, access programs that are already open or access open documents or folders.

While an item is opening, its icon bobs up and down on the Dock.

Once an item has been opened from the Dock, its applications, folders or files can be opened by double-clicking on them.

Due to the power of OS X, numerous programs can be open and running at the same time, without affecting the overall memory of your computer. This is because OS X assigns all of the available memory to the active program, i.e. the one that is being worked with. If you switch to another program, the memory is assigned to that one, and so on.

1 Click once on an item on the Dock to open it

2 The selected item opens in a new window. Each new item selected from the Dock opens in its own window

3 Once an item has been opened, a black triangle appears below it. This only disappears once the item is closed

Dock menus

One of the features of the Dock is that it can display contextual menus for selected items. This means that it shows menus with options that are applicable to the item that is being accessed. This can only be done when an item has been opened.

If the selected item is a program, any open files will be displayed in the item's Dock contextual menu. Click on a file to access it directly.

1 Click and hold here to display an item's individual menu

2 Click on Show In Finder to see where the item is located on your computer

Click on Quit on the Dock's contextual menu to close an open program or file, depending on which side of the dividing bar the item is located.

For a more detailed look at the workings of the Finder, see Chapter Three.

Trash

The Trash folder is a location for placing items that you do not want to use anymore. However, when items are placed in the Trash, they are not removed from your computer. This requires another command, as the Trash is really a holding area before you decide you want to remove items permanently. The Trash can also be used for ejecting removable disks attached to your Mac.

Items can also be sent to the Trash by selecting them and then selecting File>Move to Trash from the Menu bar.

Sending items to the Trash

Items can be sent to the Trash by dragging them from the location in which they are stored:

All of the items within the Trash can be removed in a single command: Select Finder>Empty Trash from the Menu bar to remove all of the items in the Trash folder.

1 Drag an item over the Trash icon to place it in the Trash folder

2 Click once on the Trash icon on the Dock to view its contents

If you select the Empty Trash option this removes all of the items in the Trash folder permanently. If you choose to do this, check all of the items in the Trash to make sure you are not removing something that you still need.

Adding and removing Dock items

Adding items

As many items as you like can be added to the Dock; the only restriction is the size of monitor in which to display all of the Dock items (the size of the Dock can be reduced to accommodate more icons but you have to be careful that all of the icons are still legible). To add items to the Dock:

Icons on the Dock are shortcuts to the related item, rather than the item itself, which remains in its original location.

Locate the required item and drag it onto the Dock. All of the other icons move along to make space for the new one

You can add as many items as you like to the Dock, but it will automatically shrink to display all of its items if it becomes too big for the available monitor space.

Keep in Dock

Everytime you open a new program, its icon will appear in the Dock for the duration that the program is open, even if it has not previously been put in the Dock. If you then decide that you would like to keep it in the Dock, you can do so as follows:

1   Click and hold on the black triangle underneath an open program

2   Click on Keep In Dock to ensure the program remains in the Dock when it is closed

Removing items

Any item, except the Finder, can be removed from the Dock. However, this does not remove it from our computer, it just removes the shortcut for accessing it. You will still be able to locate it in its folder on your hard drive and, if required, drag it back onto the Dock. To remove items from the Dock:

Drag it away from the Dock and release. The item disappears in a satisfying puff of smoke to indicate that it has been removed. All of the other icons then move up to fill in the space

Removing an item from the Dock, does not affect the actual item in any way. All it does is remove the shortcut to that item. It is still in its original location and its original format.

Removing open programs

You can remove a program from the Dock, even if it is open and running. To do this:

1 Drag a program off the Dock while it is running. Initially the icon will remain on the Dock because the program is still open

2 When the program is closed its icon will be removed from the Dock

System Preferences

In OS X there are preferences that can be set for just about every aspect of the program. This gives you great control over how the interface looks and how the operating system functions. To access System Preferences:

Click on this icon on the Dock or from the Applications folder in the Finder

Personal preferences

Appearance. Options for the overall look of buttons, menus, windows and scroll bars.

Dashboard & Exposé. This can be used to specify keystrokes for the different Dashboard and Exposé functions.

Desktop & Screen Saver. This can be used to change the desktop background and the screen saver.

Dock. Options for the way the Dock looks and functions.

International. Options for the language used on the computer.

Security. This enables you to secure your Home folder with a master password, for added security.

Spotlight. This can be used to specify settings for the OS X search facility, Spotlight

Hardware preferences

CDs & DVDs. Options for what action is taken when you insert CDs and DVDs.

Displays. Options for the screen display, such as resolution.

Energy Saver. Options for when the computer is inactive.

Keyboard & Mouse. Options for how the keyboard and mouse function and also keyboard shortcuts.

Print & Fax. Options for selecting printers and handling faxes.

Sound. Options for adding sound effects and playing and recording sound.

Internet & Network preferences

.Mac. Options for setting up your online .Mac membership and also for configuring your iDisk. This is looked at in more detail in Chapter Seven.

Network. This can be used to specify network setting for linking two or more computers together. This is looked at in more detail in Chapter Nine.

QuickTime. Options for configuring the QuickTime Player for playing movies and music.

Sharing. This can be used to specify how files are shared over a network. This is also looked at in Chapter Nine.

System preferences

Accounts. This can be used to allow different users to create their own accounts for use on the same computer.

Classic. Options for how the Classic environment operates when a pre-OS X program is launched.

Date & Time. Options for changing the computer's date and time.

Software Update. This can be used to specify how software updates are handled. It can be set so that updates are automatically downloaded when the computer is connected to the Internet.

Speech. Options for using speakable commands to control the computer. This can be useful for users who find it uncomfortable using the keyboard or the mouse as it enables them to perform some tasks by speech alone.

Startup Disk. This can be used to specify the disk from which your computer starts up. This is usually the OS X volume, or in some cases, a previous version of the Mac operating system.

Universal Access. This can be used to set options for users who have difficulty with viewing text on screen, hearing commands, using the keyboard or using the mouse. There are options for each of these areas which make it possible for as wide a range of users as possible to get the most out of OS X.

Desktop items

If required, the Desktop can be used to store programs and files. However, the Finder (see Chapter Three) does such a good job of organizing all of the elements within your computer that the Desktop is rendered largely redundant, unless you feel happier storing items here. The Desktop also displays any removable disks that are connected to your computer.

Icons for removable disks, i.e. Zip disks, CDs or DVDs, will only become visible on the Desktop once a disk has been inserted into the appropriate drive.

By default, the Desktop displays the Macintosh HD icon

If a removable disk is connected to your computer, double-click the Desktop icon to view its contents

Any removable disks that are connected to your computer can also be viewed by clicking on them in the Sidebar in the Finder.

Ejecting items

In previous versions of the Mac operating system, external disks could only be ejected by the slightly unusual method of dragging their icon over the Trash. However, although this still remains available it is also now possible to eject external disks directly from the Finder.

Ejecting with the Finder

Click here to eject an external disk

Volumes are any individual areas for storing data, such as the hard drive on your computer, connected networks, your iDisk or external drives such as a Zip drive or a CD.

Ejecting with the Trash is still a useful option if the Finder window is not immediately available i.e. it is minimized or hidden behind other windows.

Ejecting with the Trash

If you like the way things used to be done, you can still eject external disks by dragging them over the Trash:

Drag the disk's icon from the Desktop and drop it onto the Trash icon on the Dock. Release the mouse button when the word Eject appears

Organizing with Exposé

Exposé is a unique function within OS X that enables you to quickly organize and display all of your open files and programs. It can be applied to all of the items on your desktop or to a single specific program and its files. By default, Exposé is operated by the F (function) keys. To do this:

Organizing your desktop

Click once on any window to activate it and return it to its original size.

1 When working with a lot of files and programs, the desktop can become cluttered very quickly

Pass the cursor over an item that has been revealed by Exposé to see its name.

2 Press F9 to display all of the individual items that are open on the desktop. Press F9 again to return to the previous state

Organizing within a program

If there are a lot of open files within a single program, Exposé can be used to view all of the files on the desktop. The files are sized to accommodate them all within the available workspace. To do this:

1 In a single program, open files are stacked on top of one another

2 Press F10 to display all of the individual items that are open on the desktop. Press F10 again to return to the previous state

Press F11 to hide all of the open documents and programs on the desktop. This reveals a completely clear desktop. Press F11 again to restore all of the hidden items.

Universal Access

In all areas of computing it is important to give as many people access to the system as possible. This includes users with visual impairments and also people who have problems using the mouse and keyboard. In OS X this is achieved throughout the functions of the Universal Access System Preferences. To use these:

1 Click here once on the Dock to access the System Preferences

2 Double-click here

3 Click here for help with issues connected with visual impairment

Experiment with the VoiceOver function, if only to see how it operates. This will give you a better idea of how visually impaired users access information on a computer.

4 Click here to have the computer read what is on the screen

5 Click here to enable the onscreen text to be made larger

6 Click here to change the color of the screen display

7 Click here for help with issues connected with hearing difficulties. Settings can be made so that the screen flashes when there is a sound alert from the computer

8 Click here for help with issues connected with the keyboard. This helps with issues such as simplifying the process of pressing multiple keys at the same time and also repeated keystrokes

9 Click here for help with issues connected with the mouse. This enables users to use the numeric keypad instead of the mouse, changes the speed at which the mouse operates and also changes the size of the mouse cursor

Finder

The principal program for moving around OS X is the Finder. This enables you to access items and organize your programs, folders and files. This chapter looks at how to use the Finder and how to get the most out of this powerful tool that is at the heart of navigating around OS X.

Covers

Chapter Three

Working with the Finder

If you were only able to use one item on the Dock it would be the Finder. This is the gateway to all of the elements of your computer. It is possible to get to selected items through other routes, but the Finder is the only location where you can gain access to everything on your system. If you ever feel that you are getting lost within OS X, click on the Finder and then you should begin to feel more at home. To access the Finder:

Click once on this icon on the Dock

The Finder is always open (as denoted by the black triangle underneath its icon on the Dock) and it cannot readily be closed down or removed.

Overview

The Finder has its own toolbar, a Sidebar from which items can be accessed and a main window where the contents of selected items can be viewed:

The Action button has options for displaying information about a selected item and also options for how it is displayed with the Finder.

Forward and back buttons   View options   Action box

Search box

Static and removable volumes

Folders are displayed here

Sidebar

Main windows

Finder folders

Home

This contains the contents of your own home directory, containing your personal folders and files. OS X inserts some pre-named folders which it thinks will be useful, but it is possible to rename, rearrange or delete these as you please. It is also possible to add as many more folders as you want.

Your Home folder is a good one to add to the Dock, so that all of your own programs, folders and files are accessible with a single click.

Click here to access the contents of your Home folder

When you are creating documents OS X, by default, recognizes their type and then, when you save them, suggests the most applicable folder in your Home directory in which to save them. So, if you have created a word processed document, OS X will suggest you save it in Documents, if it is a photograph it will suggest Pictures, if it is a video it will suggest Movies, and so on. In all cases it is possible to change the default location suggested by OS X.

The Home folder contains the Public folder that can be used to share files with other users if the computer is part of a network

Applications

This folder contains some of the programs on your computer. However, by default, it is only the programs that come installed with OS X and not every program on your system. If you had programs that you used under a previous Mac operating system, these will be contained within the Applications (Mac OS 9) folder which can be accessed directly from your hard drive in the Finder. However, it is possible to add any of these programs to your Applications folder by opening the Applications (Mac OS 9) folder and then dragging items into the Applications folder.

Click here to access the contents of your Applications folder

The Applications folder is another one that is worth adding to the Dock.

Double-click on an application icon to open the relevant program. This will open in its own, new, window

Finder views

The way in which items are displayed within the Finder can be amended in a variety of ways, depending on how you want to view the contents of a folder. Different folders can have their own viewing options applied to them and these will stay in place until a new option is specified.

Back button

When working within the Finder each new window replaces the previous one, unless you open a new program. This prevents the screen becoming cluttered with dozens of open windows, as you look through various Finder windows for a particular item. To ensure that you never feel lost within the Finder structure, there is a Back button on the Finder toolbar that enables you to retrace the steps that you have taken.

If you have not opened any Finder windows, the Back button will not operate.

1. Navigate to a folder within the Finder (in this case the "For printing" folder contained within Pictures)

2. Click on the Back button to move back to the previously visited window (in this case, the main Pictures window)

Icon view

One of the viewing options for displaying items within the Finder is as icons. This provides a graphical description of the items in the Finder. It is possible to customize the way that icon view looks and functions:

Icon view is a quick way to identify what items are, i.e. programs, folders, files, etc.

1 Click here on the Finder toolbar to access Icon View

2 Select View from the Menu bar, check on "as Icons" and select "Show View Options" to access the options for customizing icon view

Even with small icon sizes, icon view can make windows look rather cluttered, particularly if they contain a lot of items.

Select one of these options to specify the icon view for a specific window or all windows within Finder

The Icon Arrangement options can be used to arrange icons into specific groups, e.g. by name or type, or to snap them to an invisible grid so that they have an ordered appearance.

Drag this slider to set the icon size

Select an option for the way icons are arranged in Finder windows (see Tip)

Select an option for the background of the Finder window

The icon size option (see previous page) can be used to increase or decrease the size of the icons within Finder windows:

A very large icon size can be useful for people with poor eyesight, but it does take up a lot of space.

Select View>Clean Up from the Menu bar to put icons back in order if they have become disorganized over a period of time and use

List view

List view can be used to show the items within a Finder window as a list, with additional information shown next to them. This can be a more efficient method than icon view if there are a lot of items within a folder: list view enables you to see more items at one time and also view the additional information:

List view is a useful option once you feel comfortable with the way that the Finder functions.

Click here on the Finder toolbar to access List view

List view can be customized to include a variety of information such as file size and date last modified. Increase the window size (click on the green window button) to see all of the currently selected options.

To see all of the List view options, select View>Show View Options from the Menu bar.

The name of each folder or file is displayed here. If any item has additional elements within it, this is represented by a small triangle next to them (see next page). Additional information in List view, such as file size and last modified date, is included in columns to the right of the file name column

If an item in List view has a small triangle next to it, click on the triangle to display the additional contents of the folder

If you cannot find any item in the Finder, try using OS X's inbuilt search facility, located within the Finder. For more details, see page 49.

Keep clicking on triangles to drill down through the folder structure. If a triangle is pointing down, this indicates that its contents are displayed below it (and indented one step). If items do not have any triangles next to them, this means that you have reached the bottom level of this particular folder structure (or a particular branch of a multi-level structure)

Column view

Column view is a useful option if you want to trace the location of a particular item, i.e. see the full path of its location, starting from the hard drive. This can help to give a better understanding of how OS X organizes the items within it.

Click here on the Finder toolbar to access Column view

Column view is a good option for seeing the full path of the location of an item, i.e. where it is in relation to other items within the OS X structure.

The Column view window moves through each level as you trace the path of an item. For instance, if an item is five levels into a folder hierarchy, Column view will move through five panels until it displays the required item.

Click on an item to see everything within that folder. If an arrow follows an item it means that there are further items to view

Finder toolbar

Customizing the toolbar

As with most elements of OS X, it is possible to customize the Finder toolbar:

1 Select View>Customize Toolbar from the Menu bar

Do not put too
many items on
the Finder toolbar,
because you may
not be able to see
them all in the Finder window. If
there are additional toolbar items,
there will be a directional arrow
indicating this. Click on the arrow
to view the items.

2 Drag items from the window onto the toolbar, or:

3 Drag the default set of icons onto the toolbar

4 Click Done

Adding items to the Sidebar

Folders, programs and files can be added to the Finder Sidebar, in a similar way to adding them to the Dock. Once this has been done they are still also available from their original location. To do this:

1 Drag an item from an open window and release it in the Finder Sidebar

When items are added to the Finder Sidebar a shortcut, or alias, is inserted into the Sidebar, not the actual item.

2 The item can be accessed from the Sidebar and it is still located in its original location

Finder search

The Finder contains a powerful search facility that can be used to search for items over the whole computer. By default, the Finder search box is located on the Finder toolbar. To use the Finder search:

1 Enter a search word or phrase here and press Enter

Try and make your search keywords and phrases as accurate as possible. This will create a better list of search results.

2 The search results are shown here. Click on an item to see further details or double-click on it to open the item

Spotlight search

In addition to the Finder search, OS X also has another searching facility in the form of the powerful Spotlight search. This is a facility that is always visible wherever you are within OS X and it uses keywords and phrases to search for documents. When it does this it searches within a range of documents, such as PDF (Portable Document Format) files, HTML files, Word files and Excel files. It is therefore an excellent device for finding documents and files regardless of where the related keyword or phrase appears. To use the Spotlight search facility:

Since the Spotlight search is always visible, it can be a quicker way to look for items than the Finder search.

Click once on the Spotlight icon. This appears at the top right of the screen, regardless of which application you are using within OS X

Enter a keyword or phrase into the search box. As soon as this is entered Spotlight starts search

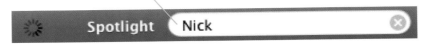

A summary of the full search results is displayed below the search box

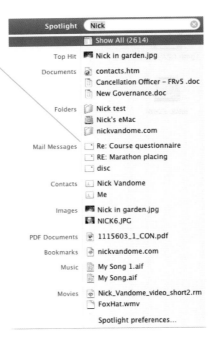

4 Double-click on an item to have it opened in its related application. For instance, a contact will be opened in the Address Book application

5 Click on Show All at the top of the summary results to see the full results. Click here to expand a category and click the "More" links to see all of the items for a specific category

6 To set Spotlight preferences, click on the "Spotlight preferences" link at the bottom of the summary of results box. Check on these boxes to include categories within the search results

If you exclude an area from Spotlight searches, make sure you remember you remember this when you are conducting subsequent searches. Otherwise you may think that an item is not there when in fact it is within the excluded area.

7 Click the Privacy tab to specify any areas on your computer over which you do not want Spotlight to perform searches. This could be because these areas contain sensitive information that you do not want anyone else to view. Click here to specify a location

8 Browse to the required location and click Choose

9 The selected location is added to the Privacy list and will be excluded when searches are performed

Creating aliases

Aliases are shortcuts to the actual version of items. This can include programs, folders and files. Aliases take up virtually no disk space and numerous aliases can be created for a single item and then placed in various locations for ease of access. To create an alias:

Select an item in any open window, by clicking on it once

2 Select File>Make Alias from the Menu bar

3 Once an alias has been created, it can then be moved to any location (in this case the Desktop)

Copying and moving items

Items can be copied and moved within OS X by using the copy and paste method or by dragging:

Copy and paste

1 Select an item and select Edit>Copy from the Menu bar

When an item is copied, it is placed on the Clipboard and remains there until another item is copied.

2 Move to the target location and select Edit>Paste item from the Menu bar. The item is then pasted into the new location

Hold down the Option key while dragging to copy an item rather than moving it.

Dragging

Drag a file from one location into another to move it to that location

Working with windows

OS X has a much better method of managing open windows than any of the previous Apple operating systems. Whenever a new item is accessed from within the Finder, it replaces the existing window, rather than opening a new window. This means that the screen does not become cluttered with a lot of open windows. The exception to this is programs, which always open in a new window.

Use the Back button to move back to the most recently accessed window.

From within the Finder, if you select a new item (except a program) it replaces the existing item, rather than opening in a new window

Program windows

As mentioned on the previous page, individual programs open up in new windows. However, it is still possible to move quickly between all open programs:

1 The currently active program is shown at the top of the open windows

2 All other windows are shown behind the active program window

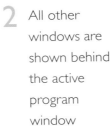

If you hold down the Command key, (the one with the Apple symbol on it), you can drag a background window without bringing it to the front.

HOT TIP

3 Click a window to bring it to the front and make it active

Working with folders

When OS X is first installed, there are various folders that have already been created to hold programs and files. Some of these are essential (i.e. those containing programs) while others are created as an aid for where you might want to store the files that you create (such as the Pictures and Movies folders). Once you start working with OS X you will probably want to create your own folders, in which to store and organize your documents. This can be done on the desktop or within any level of your existing folder structure. To create a new folder:

Access the location in which you want to create the new folder (i.e. your Home folder) and select File>New Folder from the Menu bar

Folders are always denoted by a folder icon. This is the same regardless of the Finder view which is selected. The only difference is that the icon is larger in Icon view than in List or Column views.

2 A new, empty, folder is inserted at the selected location

3 Overtype the file name with a new one. Press Enter

You can create as many "nested" folders (i.e. folders within other folders) as you want. However, this makes your folder structure more complicated and, after time, you may forget where all your folders are and what they contain.

Content can be added to an empty folder by dragging it from another folder.

4 Double-click on a folder to view its contents (at this point it should be empty)

Smart Folders

When working on any computer it is inevitable that you will soon have a number of related files in different locations. This could be because you save your images in one folder, your word processing documents in another, web pages in another and so on. This can cause difficulties when you are trying to keep track of a lot of related documents. OS X overcomes this problem through the use of Smart Folders. These are folders that you set up using Finder search results as the foundation. Then when new items are created that meet the original criteria they are automatically included within the Smart Folder. To create a Smart Folder:

Numerous different Smart Folders can be created, for different types of files and information.

1 Conduct a search with the Finder search box

2 Once the search is completed, click the Save button to create a Smart Folder

3 Enter a name for the new Smart Folder and click Save

4 The Smart Folder is added to the Finder sidebar. Click the Smart Folder to view its contents

5 Create a new item that matches the original search criteria

6 The new item is automatically included within the Smart Folder

7 Click on an item to view its full path

Creating Smart Folders from the Menu bar

In addition to creating Smart Folders from an initial search it is also possible to create them from the Finder Menu bar. To do this:

1 Select File>New Smart Folder from the Menu bar

2 Enter the criteria for the new Smart Folder and click Save

Spring-loaded folders

Another method for moving items with the Finder is to use the spring-loaded folder option. This enables you to drag items into a folder and then view the contents of the folder before you drop the item into it. This means that you can drag items into nested folders in a single operation. To do this:

The spring-loaded folder technique can be used to move items between different locations within the Finder e.g. for moving files from your Pictures folder into your Home folder.

1   Select the item you want to move

2   Drag the selected item over the folder into which you want to place it. Keep the mouse held down

Do not release the mouse button until you have reached the location into which you want to place the selected item.

3   The folder will open, revealing its contents. The selected item can either be dropped into the folder or, if there are sub-folders, the same operation can be repeated until you find the folder into which you want to place the selected item

Burnable folders

With the increasing use of images, digital video and music files, computer users are frequently copying data from their computers onto CDs. In some cases this can be a frustrating process but in OS X the use of burnable folders can make the process much quicker. These are folders that can be created specifically for the contents to be burned onto a CD. To do this:

1 In the Finder, select File>New Burn Folder from the Menu bar

2 The burn folder is created in the Finder window which was active when Step 1 was performed. Click on the folder name and overtype to give it a unique name

Applications such as iTunes and iPhoto can be used to burn CDs using the content within that application, but burnable folders are the best way to combine files from a variety of different applications and then burn them onto disks.

3 Select the items that you want to burn and drag and drop or copy and paste them into the burn folder

4 Click here to burn the CD

Selecting items

Items within OS X folders can be selected by a variety of methods:

Selecting by dragging

Drag the cursor to encompass the items to be selected. The selected items will become highlighted.

Once items have been selected, a single command can be applied to all of them. For instance, you can copy a group of items by selecting them and then applying the Copy command from the Menu bar.

Selecting by clicking

Click once on an item to select it, hold down Shift and then click on another item in a list to select a consecutive group of items.

To select a non-consecutive group, select the first item by clicking on it once, then hold down the Command key (the one with the Apple symbol on it) and select the other required items. The selected items will appear highlighted.

*The Select
All command
selects all of the
elements within
the active item.*
*For instance, if the active item is
a word processing document, the
Select All command will select all
of the items within the document;
if it is a folder it will select all of
the items within that folder.*

Select All

To select all of the items in a folder, select Edit>Select All from the Menu bar:

Labeling items

With the Finder it is possible to label items (including files, folders and programs) so that they can easily be identified for specific purposes. This could be for items that were created on a certain date or to quickly identify a particular type of document. To do this:

Labels are visible regardless of the View option that is selected in the Finder.

1 Select an item, or group of items, to which you want to apply labels

2 Click the Actions button and select a color for the label, or labels

3 The colored labels are applied to the selected items. Other items can then have other label colors applied to them

Menus

The main Apple menu bar in OS X contains a variety of menus, which are consistent regardless of the program in operation:

 Finder File Edit View Go Window Help

- Apple menu. This is denoted by a translucent blue apple and contains general information about the computer, a preferences option for changing the functionality and appearance of the Dock and options for closing down the computer

- Finder menu. This contains a preferences options for amending the functionality and appearance of the Finder and also options for emptying the Trash and accessing other programs (under the Services option)

- File menu. This contains common commands for working with open documents, such as opening and closing files, creating aliases, moving to the Trash, ejecting external devices and burning discs

- Edit menu. This contains common commands that apply to the majority of programs used on the Mac. These include undo, cut, copy, paste, select all and show the contents of the clipboard i.e. items that have been cut or copied

- View. This contains options for how windows and folders are displayed within the Finder and for customizing the Finder toolbar

- Go. This can be used to navigate around your computer. This includes moving to your Home folder, your iDisk, your Applications folder, recently opened items and also remote servers for connecting to other computers on a network

- Window. This contains commands to organize the currently open programs and files on your desktop

- Help. This contains the Mac Help files which contain information about all aspects of OS X

iLife

The term iLife refers to the programs that are bundled with OS X and which form the foundation of Apple's "digital hub" strategy. This is designed to make every aspect of digital life as easy and as user-friendly as possible. The iLife group of programs cover the areas of digital images, music (listening to and creating), video and DVDs. This chapter looks at each of these programs and shows how they can be used to enhance a digital lifestyle.

Covers

Chapter Four

iPhoto

iPhoto is the image management program for OS X. The intention of iPhoto is to make the organizing, manipulation and sharing of digital images as easy as possible. To begin using iPhoto:

1 Click once on this icon on the Dock

The Photo Library is where all downloaded images are displayed. If new albums are created and images placed into them, the images are visible in the album but they are, in effect, just a reference back to the images in the Photo Library. This means that images can be included in numerous albums without having to make several copies: each occurrence is a reference back to the Photo Library.

2 Connect your digital camera to your Mac via either USB or FireWire. The connected camera is displayed here

Check on the "Delete items from camera after importing" check box if you want images to be removed from your camera's memory card once they have been downloaded.

3 Click here to import the images from the camera. These are then displayed in the Photo Library

Viewing images

Click here to view images in different albums

Drag this slider to change
the size at which the
thumbnails are displayed

*iPhoto downloads
all of the images
held on a
camera's memory
card; there is no
facility to select specific images
before downloading.*

Click here to view selected
images as a slideshow

Creating albums

To create new albums:

*The first time that
you download
images with
iPhoto, the images
in the Photo
Library and the Last Roll folder
will be the same.*

1   Click here at the bottom of the iPhoto window

2   Enter a name for the new album

3   Click Create

4   The new album
is entered in the
folder list

Adding images to an album

Images from the main Library can be added into individual albums. However, although they are visible in these albums they are still physically located in the Library. To do this:

Select the required images and drag them into the required album

Creating slideshows

Specific slideshows can be created in a similar way to creating albums:

1. Select the required images and select File>New Slideshow from the Menu bar

Creating a slideshow in this way means that you can save it and view it again at any time. It gives you more flexibility than just selecting images and playing them in a slideshow.

2. Give the slideshow a name and it is added here

3. Click here to view the slideshow

Editing images

Although iPhoto is not a fully-featured image editing program, some editing functions can be performed, including adjusting the brightness and contrast, cropping and removing red-eye:

1 Double-click on an image to access the editing functions

2 Click here to scroll through all images

3 The editing functions can be accessed here

The Retouch tool can be used to remove small blemishes from an image. To do this, select the tool and drag over the required area on the image. The effected part will then be blended into the rest of the image.

Publishing and sharing

iPhoto has options for publishing and sharing images in a number of different ways.

Click here to access the publishing and sharing functions.
Images have to first be selected in order for them to be used in this way

The Publishing and Sharing options are excellent for ordering online prints of images and also books of prints, created with predesigned iPhoto templates.

iTunes

To open iTunes, click on this icon on the Dock:

iTunes is Apple's jukebox software that allows CDs to be played and copied onto a computer. It also allows for the burning of music onto CDs, provides access to numerous online radio stations and is an entry point to the Apple Music Store which can be used to buy music online legally. It also works seamlessly with the iPod portable music player.

Playing a CD

1 Insert a CD, which is displayed here

By default, songs are imported in the AAC format. This is an audio file format that uses high levels of compression while still retaining good sound quality. iTunes also supports downloading in MP3, AIFF and WAV formats. Select iTunes> Preferences from the Menu bar and click on the Importing tab to see all of the options for importing from a CD.

2 The individual tracks are displayed here

3 Click here to import the contents of the CD into the iTunes Library

Playlists

With iTunes you can create playlists of your favorite tracks from different CDs. To do this:

You can access names for CD tracks by selecting Advanced>Get CD Track Names from the iTunes Menu bar. However, this requires a connection to the Internet.

2   Enter a name for the playlist

1   Click here to create a new playlist

3   Select the required songs and drag them into the new playlist

If you are copying CDs with OS X, make sure that you do not misuse copyrighted material as this is illegal.

4   Click on the playlist to see its contents

iTunes and the iPod

The iPod is Apple's portable music player and it is one of the great commercial successes of the digital age. It works seamlessly with iTunes so that your entire music library can be transferred onto your iPod. Also, whenever the iPod is connected to your Mac, via a FireWire cable, recently added music is synchronized on the iPod. In addition to music, iPods can also be used to store Address Book and Calendar details. To use an iPod with iTunes:

iPods can also be updated automatically by clicking on the iPod icon in iSync and selecting the first two options, "Turn on iPod synchronization" and "Automatically synchronize when iPod is connected". For more information on iSync, see Chapter Five.

1. The connected iPod is shown here

2. The iPod can be updated manually or automatically. Once this has been done, it is shown here

3. Click here to access iPod preferences

4. Click here for general updating options

5. Click the General tab and click here to use the iPod as a hard drive for storing items such as contact addresses and calendars

iTunes Music Store

To further enhance iTunes and the iPod there is now an online iTunes Music Store that can be used to download legally a wide variety of music. To use the Music Store:

The Music Store can only be accessed via an active Internet connection.

Once you locate specific tracks in the Music Store there is an option for buying them.

1 Click here to access the Music Store

2 Click here to select the available types of music

Disk burning

Once you have downloaded music into iTunes you will be able to burn it onto a blank CD. To do this:

CDs created from the AAC format can be played on commercial CD players.

1 Copy the required items into a playlist and select the playlist

2 Click here to burn the disk

iMovie

iMovie is Apple's video editing program that can be used to edit video from a digital video camera or video that has been converted from an analog camera. Once video has been obtained, it can be edited in the same way, regardless of its original source. The first step in the process is to obtain video which can be used in iMovie.

Obtaining video from a video camera

To open iMovie, click on this icon on the Dock:

I Attach the video camera to your Mac computer. (This involves connecting it via the FireWire connection.) Drag this slider to the left to access the camera

2 Click Import

Make sure you have a FireWire connection on your computer before you start working with digital video. This is used for downloading the video onto your computer and it transfers data very quickly, which is essential for digital video and its large file sizes.

3 Clips are downloaded here, in the clip pane

4 Drag this slider to the right to enter edit mode

Adding clips

Once video clips have been downloaded they can be assembled into a project in iMovie. This is done by adding the clips to the timeline or storyboard. After this, other editing techniques can be applied, such as transitions and video effects. It is also possible to edit the video clips, to get rid of any unwanted footage.

1 Drag clips from the clip pane to the storyboard or timeline

The order in which clips are played can be edited by dragging the clips in front of, or behind, each other.

2 Click here to preview the selected clip

Timeline is a phrase that is used frequently in the world of video and animation. It refers to the entire duration of a clip and its elements. The storyboard displays each video clip as a thumbnail image.

3 Click here to toggle between timeline and storyboard modes

Trimming clips

To remove unwanted footage at the beginning or end of a clip:

1 Drag this marker to the point at which you want the clip to begin or end

2 Select Edit>Clear from the Menu bar

Cropping clips

To save specific footage in a clip:

Clips can be split into two so that they can be edited independently of one another. To do this, drag the playhead to the point at which you want to split the clip and select Edit>Split Video Clip at Playhead from the Menu bar. To restore a clip that has been split, select Advanced>Restore Clip from the Menu bar. This restores the clip to its original format, regardless of how many times it has been split.

1 Drag these markers to the points of the clip you want to retain

2 Select Edit>Crop from the Menu bar

Adding content

Various types of content can be added to video clips. These include, audio, titles, transitions between clips and special effects. To do this:

1 Select one of the options here. Most options have properties that can be set to determine how they operate

2 The selected item can be added to the timeline by dragging it onto or between existing clips

Magic iMovie

There is a function within iMovie that can be used to automatically create completed movies, even to the point of publishing them onto DVD. To do this:

The Magic iMovie function takes the video footage directly from the camera rather than after it has been downloaded into iMovie.

1 Connect your video camera to your Mac computer and turn it on

2 Select File>Make a Magic iMovie from the Menu bar

3 Specify the required settings and click Create

iDVD

To open iDVD, click on this icon on the Dock:

iDVD is a program for creating and burning professional-looking DVDs. It works most effectively with iMovie files and it can be used to add menus, titles and buttons to movies to improve their appearance and increase their functionality. The menus created with iDVD are similar in the way they look and operate to those that you will find on commercial DVDs. Menus can be used to link to different movies or they can link to different points (chapters) within a single movie. The main components of iDVD are:

If you do not have a SuperDrive connected to your Mac, you will not be able to use iDVD for creating DVDs.

Background

Movie title

Image or movie clip

iDVD controls

Creating menus

Menus are the part of a DVD that appear when it is first played. They give the user the opportunity to select which movie, or part of a movie, that they want to watch. To create a menu in iDVD you need the graphical interface, buttons linking to the movie, or movies, and the movie files themselves. To do this:

2 Click here to view the themes

3 Click once on a theme to add it as a background

1 Click here for adding content to your iDVD production

4 Click here to view available movie files

5 Click here to select a location from which to add movie files

6 Add movie files by dragging them here. By default, their title is that of the original file name

You do not have to use the default name for movie clips, as you can edit the title once it has been added.

Background music can also be added to a menu, by dragging an audio file onto the menu from the Media panel.

7 Add a movie clip or photograph here by dragging it from the relevant folder

8 Click on a text block and click here to select formatting options for the text

Burning a DVD

Once you have added all of the content, themes and menus with iDVD, you can burn it onto a DVD. This can be played back on a computer with a DVD drive or on most commercially available DVD players. To do this:

Insert a DVD into the SuperDrive. (If no disk is inserted the following warning dialog box appears)

Burning DVDs is a slow process, so it is best to have something else to do while iDVD is burning your files onto a DVD.

iDVD uses the DVD-R format of disc for burning DVDs

2 Click on the Burn button. This can be accessed at any time within iDVD

GarageBand

GarageBand is a music authoring program that can be used to create music from either computerized tracks or real instruments. Once the basic tracks have been recorded they can be mixed together or have special effects added to them.

Getting started with GarageBand

1 Click once on this icon on the Dock

By default, GarageBand files are saved in the GarageBand format which has a .band extension.

2 Enter details for the new project and click Create

GarageBand files are much smaller in size when they are saved in the GarageBand format than when they are exported into another format e.g. for use in iTunes.

Track controls

Timeline, where new tracks are entered

Record button

Add New Track button

Transport controls

Tempo and timing controls

3 Select either a Real or Software instrument and click Create

If you want to use a real instrument, such as a guitar, make sure it has an attachment such as a USB cable, to connect it to your computer.

4 A new track is created with the appropriate instrument. Use the Mixer to alter the volume of the track

5 Select Window>Keyboard from the Menu bar (the keyboard is used as the input device for software instruments)

The playhead is the red line that moves along a track as it is being played or recorded. Wherever the playhead is, that is what is heard at that point in the track.

6 Click here to start recording

7 Click on the keyboard to record individual notes

8 As the notes are played, they are recorded on the track on the timeline

Recording vocals

Vocals are treated as a real instrument in GarageBand and both of these elements are added in a similar way. To add vocals there has to be a compatible microphone attached to your Mac. To add vocals:

Use a good quality microphone to ensure the best audio quality.

2 Select Real Instrument and a Vocals option

1 Click here to create a new track

3 Click Create

Real instruments, including vocals, appear on a purple background on the timeline, instead of the green one used for software instruments.

5 The vocals are added to the timeline

4 Click here to start recording the vocal track

Using loops

Loops are pre-recorded segments of music that can be added to songs as backgrounds or used to create whole songs. To use loops:

Most pieces of looped music are fairly short initially. However, it is possible to extend them so they continue for a whole song. See next page for details of how to do this.

1   Click here to access the loops window

2   Select a loop and drag it onto the timeline

Editing tracks

Areas within a track are known as regions and these can be edited independently from the rest of the song. To do this:

1   Click here to access the editing window

2   The region can be edited by selecting individual notes and then moving or lengthening them

Extending regions

When using segments of music, particularly loops, an effective technique is to repeat part or all of a region. This can be done by extending the length of a region. To do this:

Regions can be copied, by clicking on them and selecting Edit> Copy from the Menu bar. They can then be pasted into another part of the track by selecting Edit>Paste from the Menu bar.

Move the cursor over the end of a region until a circular arrowhead appears. Use this to extend the region by dragging. The extended region is denoted by a small v shape on the timeline

Exporting songs

Once a song has been completed it can be saved, burned onto a disc or exported into iTunes. This enables it to be played on your Mac and it can also be exported to an iPod via iTunes. To export a song to iTunes, first open it in GarageBand, then:

GarageBand files are exported to iTunes in the .aif format. These cannot then be opened by GarageBand. If you want to edit the file again, open the original GarageBand file.

1 Select File>Export to iTunes from the Menu bar

2 Access iTunes. The exported song will be available in the Library

Getting productive with OS X

In addition to the iLife suite of programs, there are several other applications within OS X that can be used to create, store and display information. This chapter shows how to access and use these programs, so that you can get the most out of OS X and your Mac.

Covers

Chapter Five

Dashboard

The OS X Dashboard is a collection of widgets that can be used for common tasks such as a calendar, an address book and a dictionary. To use the Dashboard:

1. Click once on this icon on the Dock

By default, the Dashboard widgets can be accessed quickly by pressing F12.

2. The Dashboard widgets are maximized on the screen and superimposed over the rest of the active programs

Some widgets, such as the one for weather around the world, require an active Internet connection.

3. Individual widgets can be accessed while the others are still in view

4. Click here to view the panel of all of the available widgets (by default, only a selection are visible when the Dashboard is accessed)

5 The full range of widgets are shown here

BEWARE

Some widgets are specific to a particular geographical region e.g. sports scoreboards may only cover one country, or a particular sport.

6 To make a widget active, drag it from the Dashboard panel onto the main window

7 Click here to close an active widget

8 Click here to scroll through the available widgets

Dashboard preferences

Since the Dashboard contains such a useful selection of items, it is important to be able to access it as quickly as possible. This can be customized with the Dashboard and Exposé System Preferences. To do this:

1   Double-click here within System Preferences

Dashboard & Exposé

The Dashboard preferences can be used in the same way for the settings for the Exposé application.

2   Click here if you want to create active window corners for accessing the Dashboard. This means that when the cursor is positioned in the specified screen corner the Dashboard will be activated or deactivated

Preferences can be set for some individual widgets by clicking on the small "i" on the bottom right of the widget.

3   Click here to select a hot key for accessing the Dashboard. By default it is F12

Adding Dashboard widgets

In order to maximize the benefit of the Dashboard, Apple have encourage developers to create and publish their own widgets. This has resulted in dozens of new widgets that can be downloaded from the Apple website at www.apple.com/downloads/dashboard/. From here, the available widgets can be viewed and downloaded:

1 Click here to download specific widgets

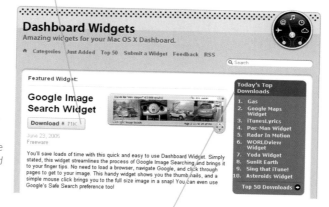

Check the Apple website regularly to see the latest widgets that have been created and are available for downloading.

2 Click here to view the top 50 downloads

3 Scroll down the downloads page and click here to view available widgets by category

Address Book

The Address Book can be used to store contact information, which can then be used in different applications and even published on the Web so that you can access it from computers around the world. The Address Book can be opened by double-clicking on the Address Book icon in the Applications folder in the Finder.

Overview

The Address Book contains contact information, either for groups or for individuals. The Address Book can display this information in two ways:

To open the Address Book, click on this icon on the Dock or in the Applications folder:

Click here to view card and column information

Address Book can import contacts in the vCard format (which uses the .vcf extension). So if you have a lot of contacts on a Windows-based PC you can export them as vCards, copy them onto a disk and import them into Address Book. To do this, select File>Import>vCards from the Menu bar and browse to the folder on the disk on which they are held.

2 Click here to view card information only i.e. individual Address Book entries

Adding contact information

The main function of the Address Book is to include details of personal and business contacts. This has to be done manually for each entry, but it can prove to be a valuable resource once it has been completed. To add contact information:

1   Click here to add a new contact

2   Click on a category and enter contact information. Press Tab to move to the next field. Click the green button to access additional options for a certain category

Different types of entries have different icons next to them. The entry for the computer's administrator is a black silhouette rather than an index card used for a standard entry.

3   Click here and browse your hard drive to add a photograph for the selected contact

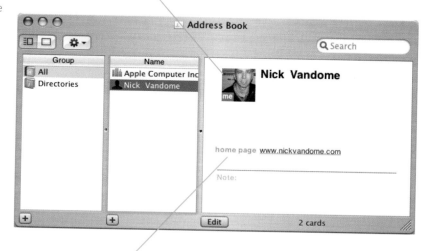

4   Contact information is shown here

Adding personal contacts

Create a new contact and enter the information here. Make sure the Company box is checked off

The search box can be used to quickly find specific entries of groups of contacts with a shared characteristic.

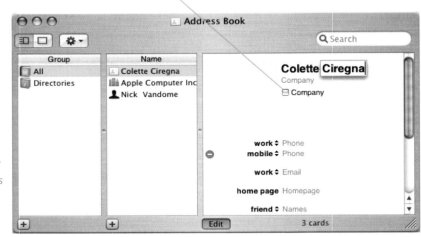

Adding business contacts

Create a new contact and check on the Company box. Business contacts and personal contacts have different icons

Creating groups

In addition to creating individual entries in the Address Book, group contacts can also be created. This is a way of grouping contacts with similar interests. Once a group has been created, all of the entries within it can be accessed and contacted by selecting the relevant entry under the Group column. To create a group:

Individual and group entries in Address Book can be used within the OS X email program, Mail. When you enter names in the email To box the relevant options from the Address Book will be displayed.

1 Click here to create a new group. Type a name for the group

Individuals can be included in several groups. However, if you change their details in one group these changes will take effect across all of the groups in which the entry occurs.

2 Drag existing contacts into the new group

3 Click on a group to view its contents

iCal

iCal is a calendar and organizer that can be used to keep track of all of your social and business appointments, important dates and To Do lists. Calendars can be created for different categories and they can even be published on the Web via a personal account with the .Mac online service. To use iCal:

To open iCal, click on this icon on the Dock or in the Applications folder:

Viewing iCal

When iCal is opened it displays the current date in the icon on the Dock.

Available calendars

Calendar content goes here

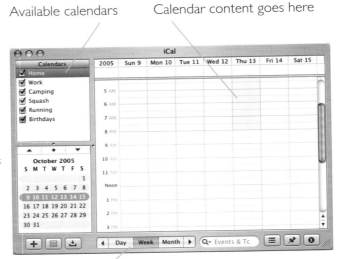

Viewing options

Click here to change the calendar view

iCal calendars can be published online using the .Mac service. To do this, open the calendar and select Calendar> Publish from the Menu bar. Once the calendar is published you will be able to send an email to people to tell them about its existence and location.

Adding calendar content

1 Click on an existing calendar

To create an all-day appointment, click on the "i" icon at the bottom right of the iCal window. In the new panel, check on the "all-day" box.

2 Click here to select a month

3 Drag on a day and enter the required text

4 To determine the look of the calendar, select iCal>Preferences from the Menu bar and select the required options

Adding calendars

Numerous calendars can be created with iCal, so you can keep track of business appointments, social events and group activities. Each calendar is color-coded and multiple calendar information can be displayed within the calendar window. To add calendars:

1 Click here to create a new calendar and type a name for it in the Calendar window

Events can be moved by dragging them from the current location to a new one, such as from day to day.

2 Enter events for the new calendar. They will appear in the calendar's default color

3 All calendar events for a selected date are displayed. If events overlap, the details of the selected calendar appear above the other calendars

To Do lists

Within iCal there is an option to add reminders via the To Do list.
To do this:

1   Select a calendar and click here to show the To Do list

Calendars and
To Do list can be
transferred onto
a mobile device
such as the iPod
using the iSync program. For more
information, see pages 102-103.

2   Select File>New To Do from the Menu bar

3   Enter details for the To Do list. Select a different calendar to add
reminders for items within it. These will appear in the designated
color for the selected calendar

Events and
To Do items
can be deleted
automatically
by iCal after the
date has passed. To do this, select
iCal>Preferences from the Menu
bar and check on the relevant
box under the "Events and To
Do Items" heading. There is also
a box to specify the number of
days items are to be kept after
the date has passed.

iSync

iSync is a small program within OS X, but one which you may grow to love. Its role is to make sure that information within the Address Book, Calendar and, where applicable, iTunes are updated and synchronized on a variety of devices and locations. These include the .Mac service, the iPod, handheld computers and cellphones. With iSync you can be sure that you are always looking at your most up to date information, regardless of where you are or the type of device on which you are viewing the data. To use iSync with different devices:

iPods can also be updated directly from within iTunes, without the need to synchronize all of the other items on your computer.

1 Click on this icon on the Dock

2 Select Devices>Add Device from the Menu bar for each device to be included in the synchronization process

3 Click on a device to select preferences for the iSync process

```
⊖ ○ ○                          iSync

   🌐        📱                              🔄
  .mac    NICK'S IPOD                      Sync Now

NICK'S IPOD
Last synchronized:  Thursday, 1 April 2004 15:42PM

☑ Turn on NICK'S IPOD synchronization

☑ Automatically synchronize when iPod is connected

☑ Contacts ─────────────────────────────

            Synchronize:  [ All contacts          ▲▼ ]

☑ Calendars ────────────────────────────

            ⦿ All
            ○ Selected:   ☑ Home
                          ☑ Work
```

4 Click here to begin the iSync process

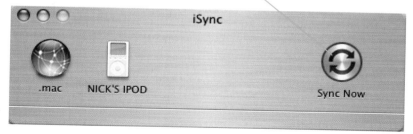

5 For some devices the update is shown within the relevant program

6 When syncing from your computer to the .Mac service for the first time, the following alert appears asking how you want the process to be handled. Once you are happy with the options, click on Sync

Font Book

The Font Book is an application that can be used to add, organize and remove fonts within OS X. To use the Font Book:

Viewing fonts

The available fonts on the system can be viewed via the Font Book:

To open the Font Book, click on this icon on the Dock or in the Applications folder:

Click on a Collection and a Font. An example is displayed here

Most computer users only use a small percentage of the fonts available to them, but it is best to keep most of them installed as you never know when you might want to use a different font.

Adding fonts

New fonts can be added through Font Book and existing fonts can be disabled throughout your computer. To do this:

1 Click here to add a new font

Fonts can be added from CDs, such as those found on the covers of computer magazines.

2 Click here to disable an existing font

Preview

Preview is an OS X application that can be used to view multiple file types, particularly image file formats. This can be useful if you just want to view documents without editing them in a dedicated program, such as an image editing program. Preview can also be used to view PDF (Portable Document Format) files and also preview documents before they are printed. To use Preview:

To open the Preview, click on this icon on the Dock or in the Applications folder:

1   Double-click on an item within the Finder

2   The selected file is displayed by Preview

If you want to edit digital images use either iPhoto or a image editing program such as Photoshop Elements from Adobe.

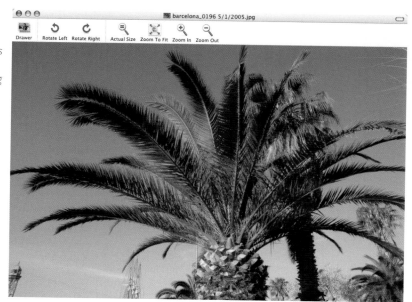

AppleWorks for OS X

AppleWorks is the Apple suite of productivity programs and it has been optimized to work effortlessly with the operating system. All iMac, iBook and eMac computers come with AppleWorks pre-installed and OS X ensures that its collection of programs work effectively and efficiently. The AppleWorks programs are:

The version of AppleWorks for use with OS X is 6.2.4 or later.

- Word Processor

- Spreadsheet

- Database

- Drawing

- Painting

- Presentation

Each of these applications function independently of the others, but it is possible to copy items from one program to another.

Opening AppleWorks

AppleWorks is usually located within the Applications folder and can be opened as follows:

Open the AppleWorks folder and double-click here to launch the program

AppleWorks documents can be saved into the equivalent Windows formats for transfer to a Windows-based PC. For instance, for a word processing document, select File>Save As from the AppleWorks Menu bar and select the required Word option under the File Format box.

2 Click here to select the standard applications

The Starting Points window can be accessed at any time within AppleWorks by selecting File>Show Starting Points from the Menu bar.

3 Select the application you want to use. A brief description appears underneath the icon

Assistants are like wizards that take you through a step-by-step process of creating certain types of documents. Templates are preset designs which can be amended for your own purposes.

4 Click here to select an AppleWorks Assistant

5 Click here to select an AppleWorks template

OS X applications

There are several useful OS X programs in the Applications folder:

Some of the applications (except those dealt with in this chapter) include:

- Automator. This can be used to automate repetitive tasks

- Chess. Play online chess against your Mac computer

Image Capture can be used to download images from a digital device, unless you have set iPhoto to be the default for performing this task.

- Dashboard. This is the set of small useful programs, known as widgets

- Dictionary. An online dictionary

- Image Capture. A program for transferring images from a digital camera or scanner

- QuickTime Player. The default application for viewing video

- Internet Connect. Settings for connecting to the Internet

- iPhoto, iTunes, iMovie, iDVD and GarageBand. These are part of the iLife suite and are covered in Chapter Four

Sherlock can be used to search for specific items on the Internet. However, some of its functions are now being overtaken by Dashboard widgets.

- Safari. The OS X specific Web browser

- Mail. The default email program

- Sherlock. The search facility for searching the Internet

- Stickies. A small program for adding note-like reminders

- TextEdit. A program for editing text files

OS X utilities

In addition to the programs in the Applications folder, there are also a number of utility programs that perform a variety of tasks within OS X. To access the Utilities:

1 Open the Applications folder and double-click on the Utilities folder

2 The available utilities are displayed within the Utilities folder

The utilities are the workhorses of OS X. They do not have the glamour of programs such as iPhoto or iMovie but they perform vital information gathering and general maintenance tasks.

- Activity Monitor. This contains information about the system memory being used and disk activity

- AirPort Admin Utility. This can be used if you have an AirPort facility on your computer, which enables you to perform wireless networking

- AirPort Setup Assistant. This sets up the AirPort wireless networking facility

- Audio MIDI Setup. This can be used for adding audio devices and setting their properties

- Bluetooth File Exchange. This determines how files are exchanged between your computer and other Bluetooth devices (if this function is enabled)

- Bluetooth Serial Utility. Part of the Bluetooth wireless setup

- Bluetooth Setup Assistant. This can be used to set up a wireless Bluetooth network. To do this, you first have to have a USB Bluetooth module connected to your computer

- ColorSysc Utility. This can be used to view and create color profiles on your computer. These can then be used by programs to try and match output color with the color that is displayed on the monitor

You may never need to use a utility like the Console, but it is worth having a look at it just to see the inner workings of a computer.

- Console. This displays the behind-the-scenes messages that are being passed around the computer while its usual tasks are being performed

- DigitalColor Meter. This can be used to measure the exact color values of a particular color

- Directory Access. This is an administration function for a network administrator. It allows them to give users access to various network services

- Disk Utility. This can be used to view information about attached disks and repair errors

- Grab. This is a utility which can be used to capture screen shots. These are images of the screen at a given point in time. You can grab different portions of the screen and even menus. The resultant images can be saved into different file formats

- Installer. This is used to install new programs and it works behind the scenes and launches automatically when you want to install a program

- Java folder. This is a folder that contains utilities that can be used to run and work with Java programs

- Keychain Access. This deals with items such as passwords when they are needed for networking

- Migration Assistant. This helps in the transfer of files between two Mac computers

- NetInfo Manager. This is a utility that contains a database with information relating to all of the users of a particular computer. This includes details of different users, servers and general network details

- Network Utility. This is a problem determination guide to see if the problem is on the workstation or the network

- ODBC Administrator. This can be used to work with databases that are ODBC (Object Database Connectivity) compliant. It can access multiple databases from a single application

- Print Setup Utility. This is used to add and configure printers and to view the status of any current print jobs

- Stuffit Expander. This is used to decompress and decode other programs, usually ones that have been downloaded from the Web

- System Profiler. This contains details of the hardware devices and software applications that are installed on your computer

- Terminal. This is used as an entry point into the world of UNIX

Printing

OS X Tiger makes the printing process as simple as possible, partly by being able to automatically instal new printers as soon as they are connected to your Mac. However, it is also possible to instal printers manually. To do this:

1 Open the Utilities folder within the Applications folder and double-click on the Printer Setup Utility

For most printers, OS X will detect them when they are first connected and they should be ready to use immediately without the need to instal any software or apply new settings.

2 Currently installed printers are displayed in the Printer List. Click here to add a new printer and follow the on-screen prompts

To share a printer over a network, select the Sharing preference within System Preferences and check on Printer Sharing under Services. Then open the Printer Setup Utility and click the Add button. Select IP Printing from the first drop-down box. Then add the IP address of the computer connected to the printer, in the Printer Address box. (The IP address can be found at the bottom of the Sharing window when the Personal File Sharing option is checked on.) The printer should then be available to anyone connected to your network.

3 Once a printer has been installed (either automatically or manually) documents can be printed by selecting File>Print from the Menu bar. Print settings can be set at this point and they can also be set by selecting File>Page Setup from the Menu bar in most programs

Creating PDF documents

PDF (Portable Document Format) is a file format that preserves the formatting of the original document and it can be viewed on a variety of computer platforms including Mac, Windows and UNIX. OS X has a built-in PDF function that can produce PDF files from most programs. To do this:

1 Open a file in any program and select File>Print from the Menu bar. Click here

PDF files can be viewed with the Preview program within the Applications folder.

2 Browse to a destination for the file and click Save

PDF is an excellent option if you are creating documents such as instruction booklets or manuals.

3 Look in the selected location to view the newly created PDF file

Faxing documents

With OS X you can fax any document as long as you have an internal or an external modem connected to your Mac. To do this:

1 Open the document you want to fax and select File>Print from the Menu bar

You can set preferences for incoming faxes within the Print & Fax System preference under System Preferences. Here you can enter a number for incoming faxes, which will be received on your computer.

2 In the Print dialog box, click the Fax button

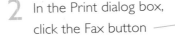

3 Enter a fax number and prefix

4 Alternatively, click here to select a recipient from the Address Book

If you select a recipient from the Address Book, make sure you have added the field for their fax number as this is the one that will be used in the To box of the Fax dialog box when a fax is sent.

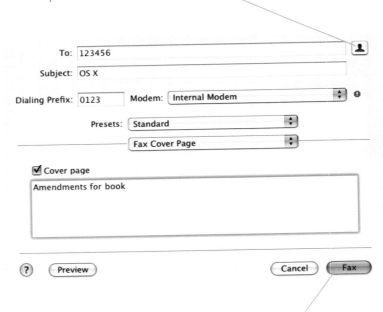

5 Enter the rest of the details of the fax, including items to be displayed on the cover page. Click the Fax button to send

Internet and email

The Internet is still one of the most rapidly developing areas of the digital world. This chapter shows how to get the most out of this vital resource. It shows various ways of connecting to the Internet and how to use the OS X Web browser, Safari and its email program, Mail. It also covers text chatting and video conferencing over the Internet and the use of RSS news feeds.

Covers

Chapter Six

Getting connected

OS X is designed very much with the Internet in mind and there are various ways to connect to the Internet through an Internet Service Provider (ISP). Once you have registered with an ISP they will send you details of how to connect to their service. This will usually include items such as your username, password and telephone number to contact when accessing their service (if using a dial-up modem). The main ways of connecting to the Internet via an ISP are a dial-up modem on a standard telephone line, a DSL (Digital Subscriber Line) connection also on a standard telephone line or a cable connection, using cables wired for television use. The latter two options come under the general term of broadband as they offer much faster connections (and therefore download speeds) than a dial-up connection. In general, broadband connections are up to 10 times faster than dial-up. Whichever connection you use, there are settings that can be applied to ensure your Internet experience works as smoothly as possible.

One option for connecting to the Internet is by using the Internet Connect program in the Applications folder.

Once you have connected to the Internet you still have to open a browser to browse the Web or an email program to send email.

Settings for a dial-up modem

1 Open System Preferences and select the Network preference

AOL users can use separate settings by selecting AOL Dial-up in the Configure box, instead of PPP.

2 Click here and select the Internal Modem option

3 Click the TCP/IP tab

4 Click here and select Using PPP

5 Click the
PPP tab

6 Enter the
account
details (these
will be
provided by
your Internet
Service
Provider)

7 Click here for
further PPP options

*Different types
of entries have
different icons
next to them.
The entry for the
computer's administrator is a
black silhouette rather than an
index card for a standard entry.*

8 Select the additional options and click OK

9 Click Apply
Now (in image
above)

Connecting via a dial-up modem

Once the settings for a dial-up modem have been applied, the Internet can be accessed in two ways:

Click here on the Apple Menu bar and select Connect

If you are having problems connecting to the Internet, select Open Internet Connect and check the relevant settings.

Select Open Internet Connect, above, (or open it from the Applications folder). This can also be used to enter a different configuration for the modem. Click Connect

Settings for an Ethernet connection

Since a DSL or cable connection via an Ethernet cable is "always on", there is no need to connect to the Internet each time you want to go online, as you do with a dial-up connection. This means that you only need to apply the required settings once and you should then be able to access the Internet via your ISP. To apply the settings for an Ethernet connection:

DHCP stands for Dynamic Host Configuration Protocol and is a method for automatically obtaining all of the details that are required to connect to the Internet. Once you click Apply Now, the settings will be obtained and applied. After this, you should be able to use your Internet connection, although you may have to reboot the computer first.

1 Open System Preferences and select the Network preference

2 Click here and select the Built-in Ethernet option

3 Click the TCP/IP tab

4 Click here and select Using DHCP

or

Settings for connecting to the Internet via an Ethernet connection can also be applied manually, in which case you would need to get the necessary information from your ISP. However, in the majority of cases, the Using DHCP option should do the trick.

if it is a PPoE connection, click here and enter the required settings which should have been provided by your ISP

5 Click Apply Now

Safari

Safari is a Web browser that is designed specifically to be used with OS X. It is similar in most respects to other browsers, but it usually functions more quickly and works seamlessly with OS X.

Safari overview

There is a version of Internet Explorer that can be used with OS X, but as Safari is designed specifically for the operating system it usually works more efficiently than the former.

1 Click here on the Dock to launch Safari

Back and forward   Refresh   Address bar   Search

Bookmarks bar

Page content

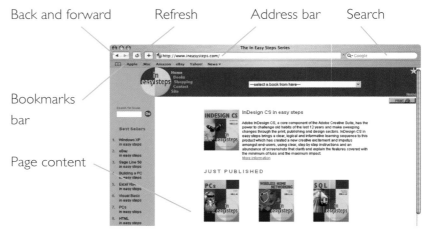

If the Address Bar is not visible, select View from the Menu bar and check on the Address Bar option. From this menu you can also select or deselect items such as the Back/Forward buttons, the Stop/Reload buttons and the Search box.

2 Select Safari> Preferences from the Menu bar to specify settings for the way Safari operates and displays Web pages

Adding bookmarks

Bookmarks are a device by which you can create quick links to your favorite Web pages or the ones you visit most frequently. Bookmarks can be added to a menu or the Bookmarks bar in Safari which makes them even quicker to access. Folders can also be created to store the less frequently used bookmarks. To view and create bookmarks:

1 Click here to view all bookmarks

 Only keep your most frequently used bookmarks in the Bookmarks Bar. Otherwise some of them will cease to be visible, as there will be too many entries for the available space.

2 All of the saved bookmarks are displayed in the Bookmarks window. Click here to add a new folder

 If you are registered for the .Mac service, you can upload all of your bookmarks to your online account and you will be able to access them from any computer with an Internet connection. For more details on this, see Chapter Seven.

3 Click here to create a bookmark for the page currently being viewed

4 Enter a name for the bookmark and select a location in which to store it

5 Click Add

Type a name for the bookmark, and choose where to keep it.

The In Easy Steps Series

Bookmarks Bar

Cancel   Add

Safari RSS

RSS, which stands for Really Simple Syndication, is a method of producing regularly updated information on websites. It works by using XML (Extensible Markup Language) and is most frequently seen on news websites: the RSS feed displays the latest news. In order for a RSS feed to be viewed, the browser has to support the RSS technology. Safari does this and when it comes across a website with RSS this icon is displayed in the Safari address bar:

Once an RSS enabled site has been located the news feeds can be accessed by clicking on the RSS icon.

RSS preferences

The way that RSS feeds are dealt with can be set within the Safari preferences by selecting Safari>Preferences from the Menu bar:

RSS is becoming increasingly popular and more and more websites are now using it for areas such as news.

Click here to access RSS settings

Specific settings can be made here

Mail

The OS X email program, simply called Mail, can be used for all standard email functions and it also has an effective system for identifying, blocking and removing junk email (spam), one of the great blights on the Internet. Before using Mail it can be useful to set a few preferences. To do this, open Mail and select Mail>Preferences from the Menu bar:

Click here to access the General preferences. These can be used to set how often Mail checks for incoming messages and also for choosing an alert sound when new mail arrives

If you have an online email account with the .Mac service, this will appear in your Mail accounts too. You can use this to download email directly from your .Mac account, without having to logon first.

If you are setting up a new email account you will need to get the details to enter from your Internet Service Provider.

Click here to view information about your current email accounts

Click here to add a new account

Receiving and sending emails

Reply to a message   Create new message   Get new mail

Mail can download messages from all of the accounts that you have set up within the Accounts preference.

Double-click here to view or disable the preview screen

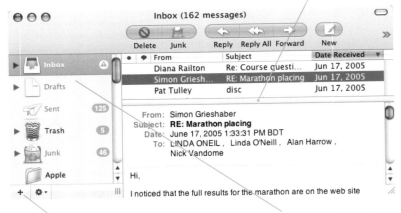

When entering the name of a recipient for a message, Mail will display details of matching names from your Address Book. For instance, if you type DA, all of the entries in your Address Book beginning with this will be displayed and you can select the required one.

Click here to create a new mailbox   Mailboxes are displayed here

Dealing with junk email

Junk email is the scourge of the Internet but it is possible to "train" Mail to identify and remove unwanted messages. To do this:

1 Select Mail>Preferences from the Menu bar and click on the Junk Mail button

2 Check on this box

Once you are content that you have trained mail to deal with junk mail, check on the "Move it to the Junk mailbox (Automatic)" option under the When Junk Mail Arrives heading. This will then automatically remove junk mail when it arrives, although it will still need to be deleted from the Trash folder manually.

3 Check on this box. This will enable Mail to build up a pattern for junk mail items

4 In your Inbox, select an item of junk mail and click here. This will help Mail identify different types of junk mail that may have escaped its own filters

Smart Mailboxes

Just as with Smart Folders (see Chapter Three) it is also possible to create Smart Mailboxes. These are mailboxes into which emails are placed if they meet certain specified criteria. This a good way to keep track of emails according to criteria such as sender or subject, or both. To create Smart Mailboxes:

1 Select Mailbox>New Smart Mailbox from the Mail Menu bar

2 Click here to select the rules for the messages to be included in the mailbox

3 Click here to add more rules

4 Numerous rules can be added for a specific Smart Mailbox

5 Click OK

6 The Smart Mailbox is added here. All messages that match the specified rules will be visible in the mailbox. However, they will still be physically located in the main Inbox

iChat

Preferences for how iChat operates can be chosen by selecting iChat> Preferences from the Menu bar.

iChat is the instant messaging service that is provided with OS X. It can be used by members of the .Mac online service or by AOL members who have access to the AOL Instant Messenger (AIM) service. iChat supports instant text messaging, telephone messaging and also video messaging (with the appropriate hardware). To use iChat:

1 Click on this icon on the Dock or in the Applications folder

A Buddy List is a list of contacts with whom you want to contact via iChat.

2 Click here to show your online status. If you select Available, this means that other people can contact you for chatting

You have to be connected to the Internet in order to be able to use iChat.

3 Click here to select an image for your online profile. This can be a graphic or a photograph of yourself

4 Click here to add a new buddy i.e. someone to chat to

5 Select a contact from your Address Book

If you choose a contact from your Address Book, they must have the details of a .Mac account entered or details of an AIM account.

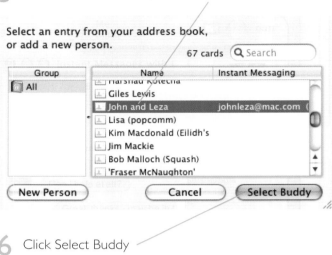

6 Click Select Buddy

7 Or, click New Person to enter the details manually

If you want to find like-minded people who use iChat, visit the website at www. ichatfinder.com/. This contains numerous contacts who are willing to participate in iChat conversations.

8 Enter the details of the new buddy contact

9 Click Add to include the contact on your Buddy List

Beginning to chat

Once you have added contacts to your Buddy List, you can start chatting with people. To do this:

1 Click on a contact on your Buddy List

If a buddy has a green circle next to their name, it means that they are currently online and available for chatting.

2 Click here to begin a text chat

The appearance of the text for your iChat conversation can be formatted in the iChat preferences.

4 The iChat conversation appears here

3 Enter text here and press Enter

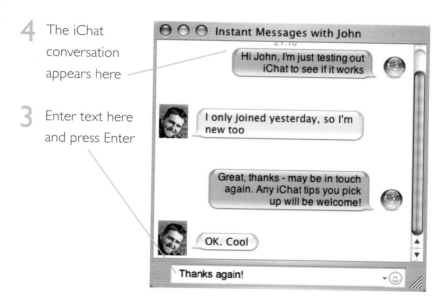

iChat AV

iChat AV operates in the same way as iChat, except that it uses video for communication rather than text. To use iChat AV you require a broadband Internet connection and the iSight video camera, that can be attached to any Mac. To use iChat AV:

Other types of webcams can be used with iChat AV, but the iSight one works most effectively and provides excellent quality.

1   Open iChat and select a buddy

2   Click here to view your own video screen

3   Click here to invite the buddy to a video chat

iChat AV allows for full screen video and audio simultaneously. This means that there is no delay in either when you are engaged in a video chat.

4   Before the video chat starts your image appears here. Once the chat starts this is minimized, but still visible, and the other person's image takes up the main part of the screen

5   Click here to select preferences for the way iChat AV operates

iChat AV can support video conferencing for up to three different users at the same time.

6   Preferences can be selected for the type of camera used, the microphone and the type of connection

Using .Mac

If you are looking for an online extension for your Mac and OS X, then .Mac is the service for you. It is an online service for Mac users that provides 250 Mb of storage space on the Internet and also a variety of functions ranging from creating Web pages to downloading valuable virus protection. This chapter shows how to join the .Mac world and use its facilities.

Covers

Chapter Seven

Registering for .Mac

Your storage space on .Mac is known as iDisk and you can also copy a version of this to your own hard drive. For more details about this, see pages 133–139.

.Mac is the online service from Apple that enables you to store files on one of the Apple computers on the Web. These files can then be accessed from any computer that is connected to the Internet and they can also be shared with other Web users. In addition to file storing and sharing .Mac also offers a variety of services:

- Online email (Mac Mail)

- Creating and publishing websites (HomePage)

- Sending electronic greetings cards (iCards)

- Publishing calendars and your address book

- File backup (Backup)

- Virus protection (Virex)

.Mac is a subscription service, but before committing yourself to this, it is possible to register for a trial period of 60 days to see how the service works and if you can make use of it. To register for the 60 day trial, go to the website at www.mac.com and click on the Test Drive .Mac link. You will need to enter some registration information such as a username and a password that can be used to access .Mac once you have registered. To register for the full service:

Whenever you log on to your .Mac account you will need to enter your password, although your member name should be pre-inserted.

1 Access the .Mac website at www. mac.com and click here to start the registration process

You must check on the "I accept the Terms and Conditions" box before you can move on to the next step of the registration process.

2 Enter your registration details and continue through the screens to complete registration

iDisk

iDisk is your own personal storage space within the .Mac service. It can be used to store files for sharing, backing up your hard drive files or storing files for use in other parts of .Mac. Once you have registered for .Mac, your iDisk will be activated. Once this has been done, you can access it by selecting Go>iDisk>My iDisk from the Finder Menu bar. As long as you are connected to the Internet, the iDisk icon will be displayed in the Finder and also on your Desktop. When you disconnect from the Internet, the icon will disappear from the Desktop, but it will remain in the Finder. By default, items can only be added to the iDisk when you are connected to the Internet.

You can view more information about your iDisk, such as how much storage space you have used up, and apply various settings within the .Mac preferences in System Preferences.

1 The iDisk icon is displayed as a separate volume in the Finder

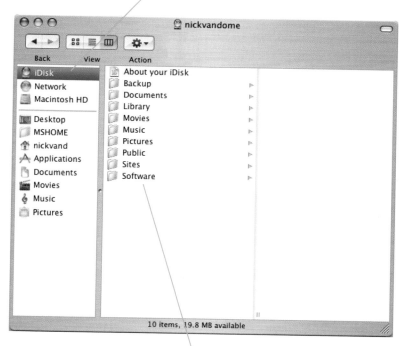

2 There are separate folders within iDisk and they are displayed here

Adding files to iDisk

Within iDisk there are nine folders. Three of these, Backup, Library and Software, are read-only folders for use with the .Mac service. The Public folder is for sharing files over the Internet. The remaining folders can all have files added to them from your hard drive. To do this:

The folders which can be used to store your own files are Documents, Pictures, Movies, Sites and Music. The Pictures folder is used by .Mac for items requiring images (such as iCards) and the Sites folder is used for Web pages by the HomePage function on .Mac.

1 Select files in the Finder and drag them over the iDisk icon and hold the mouse until the iDisk opens

2 Hold the files over the required folder until it opens. Drop the files into the open folder

Documents can also be saved directly to the iDisk from any application by using the Save As command and then selecting the required folder within iDisk as the destination.

Creating a local copy of iDisk

By default, you have to be connected to the Internet in order to access your iDisk and add files to it. However, it is also possible to create a copy of the iDisk on your own hard drive. This is known as a local copy and it enables you to add files to your iDisk even when you are not connected to the Internet. Then, when you do connect, the local version can automatically be synchronized with the remote copy on the .Mac site so that they both contain the same items. To do this:

If you are unsure about synchronizing your iDisk, check on the Manually box for the synchronize option. When you have synchronized using this method you can then apply the Automatically setting.

1 Access System Preferences from the Dock and select the .Mac preference. Check this box on for automatic syncing

2 The presence of a local version of iDisk is denoted by this icon

3 When a connection is made to the Internet the local and remote versions of iDisk are synchronized i.e. any items that have been added to the local version are copied to the remote version

If you have a dial-up connection to the Internet it could take a long time to upload certain items to your online iDisk, particularly for large documents or high resolution image files.

Sharing with iDisk

As soon as you connect to the Internet you have access to the contents of your remote iDisk (if you have created a local copy then you will have access to this regardless of whether you are connected to the Internet or not). In addition, you can also access the contents of the personal folders within your iDisk from any computer (Mac or PC) that has an Internet connection. To do this, visit the .Mac website at www.mac.com and enter your .Mac login details. You will then have access to the .Mac services and you will be able to use the files on your iDisk as required.

As well as using your own iDisk files on the Web, it is also possible to let other people share them. This means that you can distribute a variety of files such as pictures, movies and large documents without having to email them to people. The process of sharing iDisk files consists of two main steps:

● Adding files to the Public folder within iDisk

● Ensuring that the intended recipient has the required utility to enable them to view the Public folder on your iDisk

To do this:

Add files to the Public folder of your iDisk. If necessary, synchronize your local and remote versions to ensure that the new files are available over the Internet

2 For the person who is going to share the files, go to the .Mac website at www.mac.com and click here

3 Click on the link for accessing the relevant utility (there is one for use on a Mac and also a Windows version – the

The cross-platform advantage
In addition to the Mac platform, you can also open your iDisk using Microsoft Windows XP, Windows 2000 or Windows 98. As a result you can use the Documents folder in your iDisk, for instance, for files you need to touch at both work and home or when you don't have access to a Mac. For added convenience there's even a downloadable iDisk Utility for Windows XP that makes opening your iDisk on a Windows XP machine especially quick and easy.

example here is for the Windows version)

If you are downloading the iDisk utility you do not have to login to the .Mac service, so anyone can do it, not just .Mac members.

4 Click on the link to download the required utility

The iDisk utility is very small and only takes a couple of minutes to download, even if you are using a dial-up modem connection.

For Windows, the default location for the utility once it has been installed is Program Files>.Mac Utilities> iDisk Utility for Windows.

5 Click Save to download the utility to your hard drive. For ease of use, this can be the desktop. Then double-click on the utility's icon to install it

6 Open the folder in which the utility is located and double-click on its icon to open the program

If you want to access your own iDisk from another computer, check on the iDisk box and enter your .Mac password. If someone else is accessing your iDisk they will only be able to access the Public Folder within your iDisk. For this they will require your .Mac member name but not the password.

7 Check on the Public Folder button, enter the member name of the .Mac account and click Connect

8 A confirmation box states that the Public Folder has been mounted. This means it is available to view from your computer. Click OK

When items are viewed on your iDisk they can be copied onto other user's computers with the Copy and Paste commands.

9 The Public folder is displayed as a Network Drive in Windows Explorer. Double-click to view its contents

For Mac users, the relevant Disk Utility is downloaded and installed into the Utilities folder.

.Mac services

There are a number of useful services that can be accessed from the .Mac site. These include:

- Mail. This is an online email service that can also be used with the Mail application in OS X. Through the use of iSync it is possible to synchronize your .Mac mail service with your OS X one

- Address Book. If used with iSync, your Address Book contacts can be copied onto .Mac and so you always have up to date access to your contacts, as long as you have access to a computer with an Internet connection

- Bookmarks: When you bookmark your favorite websites in Safari these are not static: they can be copied to .Mac and so they are always available from any Internet enabled computer

- HomePage. This is the .Mac facility for creating and publishing your own web pages. There are numerous templates that can be used to create pages and you can then publish them to your own .Mac web space. You can also create your own pages using HTML and publish them on .Mac

- iCards. This is a .Mac service for sending online cards. You can either use the pre-designed cards or use your own images stored on your iDisk

For a lot of .Mac functions, such as synchronizing items, settings can be applied within the .Mac preferences within the System Preferences:

Backup

Backup is a program that can be downloaded from .Mac and used to backup your data to a variety of locations. This can be any folder on your hard drive, an external device (such as an external hard drive or even an iPod) or your iDisk on the .Mac server. To download Backup:

1 Click here on the .Mac homepage

Backup is only available with a full .Mac membership, rather than the trial version.

2 Click here and follow the downloading instructions

Using Backup

If you are backing up to iDisk, the maximum amount of data that you can include is 250 Mb. If the selected items exceed this limit a red bar will appear at the top of the Backup window.

1 Open Backup from the Applications folder

2 Click here to select a destination for the backed up data

3 Check the items you want to back up

4 Click here to add more items to the back up list

5 Click Backup Now to backup the selected items

Virex

Virex is a powerful antivirus program that previously has been available on .Mac. However, at the time of writing only updates to existing versions are available. To use these:

Only version 7.2 of Virex works with Tiger.

| Click here on the .Mac homepage and follow the link for Virex DAT Files

Member Central

2 Click here and follow the downloading instructions

When you first run Virex, you may be asked to update the program's virus definitions. This is to ensure that it is as up to date as possible. These are known as eUpdates and the program will be updated frequently in this way.

Using Virex

| Open Virex from the Applications folder

2 Click here to select a volume or a folder over which you want to scan

Click on the Virus Info button to get up to date information about the latest viruses.

3 Click here to scan over the selected item

4 Results are shown here

Sharing OS X

This chapter looks at how OS X can be used to allow multiple users access to their own individual working environment on the same computer. It shows how to set up different user accounts and how to customize your workspace.

Covers

Chapter Eight

About user accounts

OS X enables multiple users to access individual accounts on the same computer. If there are multiple users, i.e. two or more, for a single machine, each person can sign on individually and access their own files and folders. In addition, they can also access their own system settings and customize their workspace in exactly the way they want. This means that each person can have their own individual style for the desktop, the Dock and the Finder. When they log out and someone else logs in, the new user's preferences will be available, in exactly the same way as they left them the last time they used the computer. This form of access is known as user accounts and OS X remembers the settings and preferences for each individual user. To access and create user accounts:

Open the System Preferences and
click on the Accounts preference

Every computer with multiple users has at least one main user, also known as an administrator. This means that they have greater control over the number of items that they can edit and alter. If there is only one user on a computer, they automatically take on the role of the administrator. Administrators have a particularly important role to play when computers are networked together. Each computer can potentially have several administrators.

Adding users

Once the Accounts preference has been accessed it is possible to add, delete and edit details about users. To add a new user:

1   Existing users are listed here

There is always at least one user listed on a computer running OS X. These details are taken from the registration information that was entered when OS X was first installed.

2   Click here to add details of a new user

3   With the Password tab selected, enter the name and login details of the new user

Your shorthand name is created automatically as a contraction of your full name. However, you can change this if you want, by highlighting and overtyping the shorthand name.

4   Click the Picture tab and select an image for the new user. Click Edit to browse your hard drive to use one of your own images

If an administrator forgets their password, insert the OS X CD while holding down the C key. Once this opens, select Installer>Reset Password from the Menu bar. Then select the correct user and enter a new password. Click on Save to apply the changes.

5   If required, click the Parental Controls tab to set controls for the new user

For more information about Parental Controls, see page 151.

Deleting users

Once a user has been added their name appears on the list in the Accounts preference dialog box. It is then possible to edit the details of a particular user or delete them altogether. To do this:

1 Select a user from the list

Always tell other users if you are planning to delete them from the system. Don't just remove them and then let them find out the next time they try to login. If you delete a user, their personal files are left untouched and can still be accessed.

2 Click here to remove the selected person's user account

3 A warning box appears to check if you really do want to delete the selected user. If you do, click on Delete Immediately

Fast user switching

If you do not want to go through the process of logging in and out every time that a new user accesses the computer there is also a function for fast user switching. The only drawback of this is that it is not as secure as each user logging out each time someone else wants to use the computer. However, in the majority of cases, this will not be a great issue. To use fast user switching:

1 Open the Accounts preference window under System Preferences

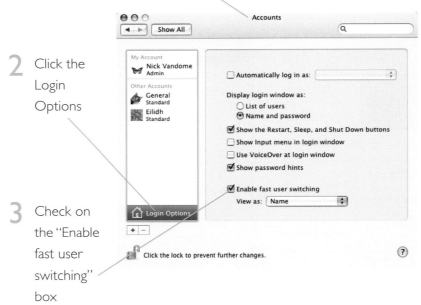

2 Click the Login Options

3 Check on the "Enable fast user switching" box

4 A warning box appears. Click OK to continue

5 The current user is displayed at the top right of the Menu bar. Click here to display other available users

6 Select another user and enter their password

Mac OS X
Nick Vandome's eMac

Eilidh

Password: ••••••••

Cancel

Log In

7 Click Log In to log in the new user and enable them to use their own personal settings on the computer

Viewing user accounts

It is possible for individual users to see the overview of another user's account. They can also exchange files with other users by placing them in a folder called a Drop Box. This means that the user can then access these files the next time they log in to their own account. (Under normal circumstances they would not be able to view any folders or files in someone else's account). To view another user's folders and share files in the Finder:

1 Select hard drive and double-click on the Users folder

The Users folder also contains the folders of any users that have been deleted.
This is where their documents are stored. A system administrator would be able to access these documents and return them to their owner, if required.

Double-click the Public folder in another user's folder. This contains the Drop Box, into which you can put files for sharing.

2 Double-click on another user's folder to view its contents

3 Folders with a No Entry icon indicate that they cannot be accessed

OS X for the family

Many families share their computers between multiple users and with the ability to create different accounts in OS X each user can have their own customized workspace. However, if children are using the computer parents may want to restrict access to certain types of information that can be viewed, particularly in relation to the Internet and email. Controls can be set within the Accounts system preference. To do this:

1 Access the user Accounts as shown on page 144

2 Click on a username and click here to access the Parental Controls

HOT TIP
To check which sites have been viewed on a Web browser, check the History menu, which is located on the main Menu bar.

3 Click here to select an application to which you want to apply controls

4 Click here to add specific rules for the selected application

5 Click OK

OS X for Windows users

Sharing files between computers is now a common feature and in OS X it is possible to share files between Mac and Windows users. To do this:

1 Double-click here in the System Preferences window

Sharing

A lot of file formats can be opened on both Macs and Windows PCs. Even Word, Excel and Powerpoint files can be exchanged, as long as each user has the relevant version of Office.

2 Click on the Services tab and check on the Windows Sharing box

3 If there is more than one user account on the computer, click here to select which account is enabled for sharing with Windows users

4 Select the required user account and click Done

5 The user account is set up for sharing with Windows users until the Stop button is clicked

Advanced features

For users that want to delve a bit more deeply into OS X there are some elements that will keep the most inquisitive computer enthusiast happy. This chapter looks at a few of these elements such as the programming language AppleScript, the Automator and also how to create a network, share files and share an Internet connection.

Covers

Chapter Nine

AppleScript

AppleScript is a programming language which can be used to write your own programs to run on a Mac computer. These can be complex applications or they could be simple utility programs. In addition to writing your own AppleScript, OS X also comes bundled with various scripts that have already been created. These can then be used on your Mac computer. To access the AppleScript options:

Even for non-programmers, AppleScript is a viable option for creating simple programs within OS X.

| In the Applications folder, double-click on the AppleScript folder

A good way to gain a general understanding of AppleScript is to look at some of the scripts in the Example Scripts folder and then open them in Script Editor (double-click on the script name in the Example Scripts folder to open it in Script Editor). This will enable you to see how the scripts are created and the syntax they use.

2 The available AppleScript options are available in the folder

Launching scripts

To launch existing AppleScripts:

1 Double-click on the Example Scripts folder

Some AppleScripts are more useful than others. Experiment with different ones to see which best fit your own needs.

2 Double-click on a script folder

3 Double-click on a script to open it

4 The script is displayed in
the Script Editor

5 Click Run to
execute the script.
An information box
describes the action
of the script. Click
Continue

6 Once the script is
run, the results are
displayed in the relevant
application, according to
the type of script

Writing scripts

If you have some programming knowledge you may want to create your own AppleScripts. To do this:

1 Open the AppleScript folder and double-click on the Script Editor

For more information about AppleScript, have a look on the Apple website at www.apple.com/applescript/

2 Write the required AppleScript. At this point it will look like plain, unformatted, text

3 Click the Compile button. This will check the syntax of the script and format it according to the items that have been entered

4   If there is a problem with the script, the Compiler will display an
    error message. Click OK to return to the script and correct the
    syntax error

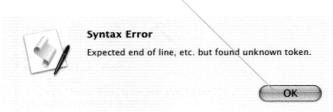

Syntax Error
Expected end of line, etc. but found unknown token.

OK

*If a script is saved
as an application
it can execute
automatically i.e.
it runs when it is
opened. If a script is saved as a
script, it has to be run manually
once it has been opened.*

5   Select File>Save
    from the Menu
    bar. Select
    either Script or
    Application as the
    file format

6   Click Save

7   Scripts are denoted
    by this icon

8   Applications are
    denoted by this icon

Using scripts

Once scripts have been created and saved they can either be run manually or automatically.

Using scripts manually

Save the script as an application and double-click on it in its folder or add it to the Finder Sidebar and single click on it here

Using scripts automatically

1 Open System Preferences and select the Accounts preference. Click on the Login Items tab and click here

2 Browse to the required script and click Add to include it in the startup process. The script will then run when the computer is booted up

Automator

Automator is an OS X application that can be used to automate a series of repetitive tasks, such as renaming a folder full of images. It works by creating a workflow of tasks, which can then be applied to a specified list of folders or files. There are numerous Automator functions that are included with the application and developers are adding more constantly. To create a workflow in Automator:

1 Double-click on this icon in the Applications folder or click on it once if it has been added to the Dock

2 This panel contains details of applications to which certain Automator tasks can be applied. Click on one to show its tasks

New Automator workflows can be downloaded from the Apple website at:

www.apple.com

3 Click here to select an action for the workflow

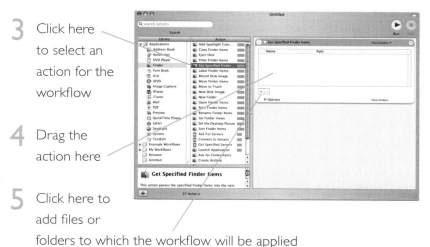

4 Drag the action here

Numerous actions can be added to a single workflow. However, make sure that you want all of the actions to be applied to all of the selected files or folders.

5 Click here to add files or folders to which the workflow will be applied

6 Select the required files and click Open

7 Add other actions to the workflow as required

8 Click here to set the specific criteria for an action within the workflow

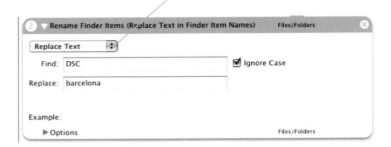

9 Click here to run the workflow i.e. have it applied to the selected folders or images

Depending on the processes involved and the number of steps, it can take a few minutes to execute an Automator workflow.

10 The completed workflow is indicated here

11 Check the source files to check that the workflow has been applied as expected

Automator workflows can also be created by first selecting the required folders or files, then Ctrl+click and selecting Automator from the contextual menu.

12 Once the workflow has been completed, select File>Save from the Automator Menu bar to save it. This will keep it for future use and also ensure that the changes made are permanent

Networking overview

Before you start sharing files directly between computers, you have to connect them together. This is known as networking and can be done with two computers in the same room, or with thousands of computers in a major corporation. If you are setting up your own small network it will be known in the computing world as a Local Area Network (LAN). When setting up a network there are various pieces of hardware that are initially required to join all of the required items together. Once this has been done, software settings can be applied for the networked items. Some of the items of hardware that may be required include:

If you have two Macs to be networked and they are in close proximity then this can be achieved with an Ethernet crossover cable. If you have more than two computers, then this is where an Ethernet hub is required. In both cases, there is no need to connect to the Internet to achieve the network.

- A network card. This is known as a Network Interface Card (NIC) and all recent Macs have them built-in

- An Ethernet port and Ethernet cable. This enables you to make the physical connection between devices. Ethernet cables come in a variety of forms but the one you should be looking for is the Cat5E type as this allows for the fastest transfer of data. If you are creating a wireless network then you will not require these

- A hub. This is a piece of hardware with multiple Ethernet ports that enables you to connect all of your devices together and let them communicate with each other. However, conflicts can occur with hubs if two devices try and send data through it at the same time

- A switch. This is similar in operation to a hub but it is more sophisticated in its method of data transfer, thus allowing all of the machines on the network to communicate simultaneously, unlike a hub

Once you have worked out all of the devices that you want to include on your network you can arrange them accordingly. Try and keep the switches and hub within relative proximity of a power supply and, if you are using cables, make sure they are laid out safely.

It is perfectly possible to create a simple network of two computers by joining them with an Ethernet cable and applying the software settings shown on page 166.

Ethernet network

The cheapest and easiest way to network computers is to create an Ethernet network. This involves buying an Ethernet hub or switch, which enables you to connect several devices to a central point, i.e. the hub or switch. All Apple computers and most modern printers have an Ethernet connection, so it is possible to connect various devices, not just computers. Once all of the devices have been connected by Ethernet cables, you can then start applying network settings (see page 166).

AirPort network

The other option for creating a network is an AirPort network. This is a wireless network and there are two main standards used by Apple computers: AirPort, using the IEEE 802.11b standard, which is more commonly known as Wi-Fi, which stands for Wireless Fidelity and the newer AirPort Extreme, using the newer IEEE 802.11g standard which is up to 5 times faster than the older 802.11b standard. Thankfully AirPort Extreme is also compatible with devices based on the older standard, so one machine loaded with AirPort Extreme can still communicate wirelessly with an older AirPort one.

One of the issues with a wireless network is security since it is possible for someone with a wireless-enabled machine to access your wireless network, if they are within range. However, in the majority of cases the chances of this happening are fairly slim, although it is an issue about which you should be aware.

The basics of a wireless network with Macs is an AirPort card (either AirPort or AirPort Extreme) installed in all of the required machines and an AirPort base station that can be located anywhere within 150 metres of the AirPort enabled computers. Once the hardware is in place, wireless-enabled devices can be configured by using the AirPort Setup Assistant utility found in the Utilities folder. After AirPort has been set up the wireless network can be connected. To do this, open the Internet Connect application and select AirPort from the toolbar. Then select an available network and click Connect. All of the wireless-enabled devices should then be able to communicate with each other, without the use of a multitude of cables.

Another method for connecting items wirelessly is called Bluetooth. This covers much shorter distances than AirPort and is usually used for items such as printers and cellphones. Bluetooth devices can be connected by using the Bluetooth Setup Assistant in the Utilities folder.

Network settings

Once you have connected the hardware required for a network, you can start applying the network settings that are required for different computers to communicate with one another. To do this (the following example is for networking two Mac computers):

1 In System Preferences, double-click on the Network icon

Network

2 Click here and select the Built-in Ethernet option

TCP/IP stand for Transmission Control Protocol/ Internet Protocol and is a protocol that enables computers on a network or the Internet to communicate and understand one another.

3 Click on the TCP/IP tab (this contains settings that help determine how computers communicate with each other)

4 Click here and select Manually

Each computer that you want to include on a network has to have its own unique IP address.

5 Enter the computer's IP address here. This is a series of four sets of three numbers. Use 192 and 168 for the first two sets and numbers between 0 and 255 for the second two sets

6 Enter 255.255.255.0 for the Subnet Mask

7 Click Apply Now

Connecting to a network

You can also connect to another Mac over the Internet by obtaining their public IP address and entering this in the Connect to Server dialog box. To find out a computer's public IP address, select the Sharing preference and click on Personal File Sharing. The IP address should be at the bottom of this window.

Once network settings have been applied to all of the computers that are going to use the network you can then connect them together and create a network. To do this:

1 In Finder, select Go>Connect to Server from the Menu bar

2 Enter the IP address of the computer to which you want to connect

When connecting to a local network, the IP address that is used is known as a personal IP address. This means that it is not being used over the Internet. Computers on different networks can use the same private IP addresses as long as they are not going to come in conflict with one another.

3 Click Connect

4 Select an option for how you want to connect to the networked computer and enter any required details

IP addresses for connecting to the Internet are known as public IP addresses and they are unique to ensure that no two devices are trying to use the same address.

5 Click Connect

If you connect to another computer as a guest, you will only be able to access certain parts of the system.

6 Select the part of the networked computer to which you want access

7 Click OK

8 The networked computer shows up as a new volume in the Finder. If you are the administrator of both machines, you can access the files on the networked machine in the same way as if you were operating that machine

If your network connection does not show up as expected, check that you have enabled Personal File Sharing. See next page for details.

You can disconnect from a networked computer by ejecting it in the Finder in the same way as you would for a removable drive such as a DVD.

File sharing

The main reason for creating a network is being able to share files between different computers. Once the network is up and running there are various options for doing this:

1 In System Preferences, double-click on the Sharing icon

Sharing

2 Click on the Services tab to view the options for sharing files

3 Check the Personal File Sharing box on to enable other networked computers to share files on your machine

Sharing with public folders

If you want to share some of your files with another user but not give them access to the whole of your computer, this can be done by placing items into a public folder. This can then be accessed by other users (guests) that are networked to your computer. To do this:

If another user is having problems accessing the files in your Drop Box, check the permissions settings that have been assigned to the files. See Chapter Ten, page 185 for further details.

1 In Finder, select your own home folder and double-click on the Public folder

The contents of the Drop Box can be accessed by other users on the same computer as well as users connected via a network.

2 Double-click on the Drop Box

3 Place the files you want to
share in the Drop Box

*It is best to copy
files into the Drop
Box rather than
moving them
completely from
their current location.*

4 From the other
computer, connect
to the required
machine on the
network

5 Select the required volume
and click OK

*Set permissions
for how the Drop
Box operates
by selecting it in
the Finder and
Ctrl+clicking on it. Select Get Info
from the subsequent menu and
apply the required settings under
the Ownership & Permissions
heading.*

6 Browse to the Drop Box and
view or copy the files that
have been placed there

Wireless networking

Networks can be created with computers connected with cables, but a more flexible method is to create a wireless network. This means that the networked computers can easily be moved around, as long as they are within range of the wireless base station. The base station is the device that is the center of the wireless network and in order to operate with it each networked computer has to have a wireless network card installed. With OS X both AirPort and AirPort Express base station can be used to create a wireless network between two or more wireless enabled Mac computers. Once the base station has been plugged in it has to be configured so that the computers can recognize it. To do this:

1 Double-click the AirPort Setup Assistant icon in the Utilities folder

If a network card is installed in a Mac computer, it should automatically be able to identify a new base station once it is plugged in.

2 Click Continue to start the setup process

3 Click here to set up a new base station

4 Click Continue

5 If a base station is not found automatically, click here to scan for one that is within range of the computer

6 Click Continue to complete the configuration process

Accessing the Internet wirelessly

Once you have set up your wireless network, it can also be used to connect to the Internet. To do this:

1 Open the Network preferences

2 Click here and select your wireless base station

3 View the required settings here

Sharing an Internet connection

Cable/DSL routers can be used to access the Internet through a dial-up connection, not just for cable or DSL access.

Once you have created a network of two or more computers it can be a considerable benefit to be able to share an Internet connection between them. This means that two, or more, people can use a single Internet connection at the same time.

Hardware method of sharing

One way to share an Internet connection is to use a device known as a cable/DSL router. This is connected to your Internet connection at one end and all of your networked computers at the other through Ethernet cables (providing there are enough Ethernet ports for all of your machines). The router serves the role of connecting the Internet and all of the networked machines.

Software method of sharing

If you have two computers networked via an Ethernet cable, the router serves as the connection between them: each machine has a cable that attaches to the router.

Using OS X it is also possible to share an Internet connection from one computer to others on your network To do this, connect your computer to your Internet connection at one end, via an Ethernet cable or to a dial-up modem. Then, connect the computer with the Internet connection to another machine (or a hub or switch if you want to share it with more than one machine.) The relevant software settings can then be applied in the Sharing preference within System Preferences:

If you are sharing a cable or DSL Internet connection with the software method, the computer connecting to the Internet requires two Ethernet ports, one for the Internet connection and one to connect to the rest of the network.

1 Click on the Internet tab

2 Select an option here

3 Click Start to begin Internet sharing

Maintaining OS X

Even though OS X lives up to the claim of being extremely stable, it still benefits from a robust maintenance regime. This chapter looks at some of the tasks that can be performed to keep OS X in top shape and it also covers some general troubleshooting issues that could occur.

Covers

Chapter Ten

Disk Utility

Disk Utility is a utility program that allows you to perform certain testing and repair functions for OS X. It incorporates a variety of functions and it is a good option for general maintenance and if your computer is not running as it should.

Each of the functions within Disk Utility can be applied to specific drives and volumes. However, it is not possible to use the OS X start-up disk within Disk Utility as this will be in operation to run the program and Disk Utility cannot operate on a disk that has programs already running. To use Disk Utility:

Disk Utility is located within the Applications> Utilities folder.

Checking disks

Click the First Aid tab to check a disk

The start-up disk is automatically checked when OS X is booted up.

Disk Utility is a good way to see how much space is left on a specific disk.

2 Select a disk and select one of the first aid options

Erasing a disk

To erase all of the data on a disk or a volume:

1 Click on the Erase tab and select a disk or a volume

If there is a problem with a disk and OS X can fix it, the Repair button will be available. Click on this to enable Disk Utility to repair the problem.

2 Click Erase to erase the data on the selected disk or volume

If you erase data from a removable disk, such as a pen drive, you will not be able to retrieve it.

Partitioning a disk

To create additional partitions on a disk or a volume:

1 Click on the Partition tab and select a disk or volume

2 Select options for partitioning

Partitions are separate areas within a disk or volume. This does not change the overall size of the item but it can help to organize your data.

3 Click Partition

System Profiler

System Profiler is a utility program that can be used to view information about the hardware and software installed on your computer. It can give valuable information about how your system is running and if there are any problems with any elements of your computer. To use System Profiler:

System Profiler is located within the Applications> Utilities folder.

1 Click here to obtain details of internal and external hardware devices

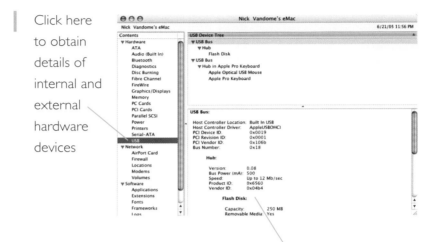

2 Details of hardware devices are displayed here

3 Click here to obtain details of software programs on your computer

4 Details of software programs are displayed in the main window

Activity Monitor

Activity Monitor is a utility program that can be used to view information about how much processing power and memory are being used to run programs. This can be useful to know if certain programs are running slowly or crashing frequently. To use Activity Monitor:

1 Click here to see how much processing power a certain application is using

Activity Monitor is located within the Applications> Utilities folder.

Select the Network tab to see how your network connection is operating i.e. how much data it has downloaded and the speed of the connection.

2 Click here to see how much system memory is being used while a certain application is in use

Updating software

Nothing in the world of computing stands still for long and this is particularly true of software, which is being updated continually. To make sure that you always have the latest versions of the Apple programs on your system it is possible to have updates sent to your computer as they are released. To do this:

1   In System Preferences, double-click on the Software Update icon

In a lot of cases, software updates will be downloaded and installed automatically.

2   Set the preferences for obtaining software updates automatically. Click Check Now for recent updates

For some software updates, such as those to OS X itself, you may have to restart your computer for them to take effect.

3   Once an update has been downloaded, double-click on this icon to access the installation folder

Virex_7.5.1.dmg

4   Double-click here to install the program or update

Restoring preferences

One factor that can cause problems with a program is if its Preferences folder becomes corrupted. This was a particular problem with OS 9 and earlier, but it can still occur with OS X. If a program is crashing a lot then you can try removing its Preferences folder and closing down the program. The next time it is opened, OS X will create a new Preferences folder that should be corruption free. To do this:

The problem of corrupted Preferences folders is a lot less common in OS X than in earlier versions of Mac operating systems.

1 Click on the Finder icon on the Dock and click on your Home folder

2 Double-click on the Library folder

3 Double-click on the Preferences folder

4 Select the Preferences folder of the program that is causing problems

If you have several programs running when a problem occurs, delete all of the relevant Preferences folders in turn. After deleting each one, open the programs to see if the problem has been resolved. If not, repeat the process with another Preferences folder. In this way you should be able to isolate the program with the problem. After each Preferences folder has been removed to the Trash, you will have to reboot your computer so that OS X can create a new Preferences folder for that program.

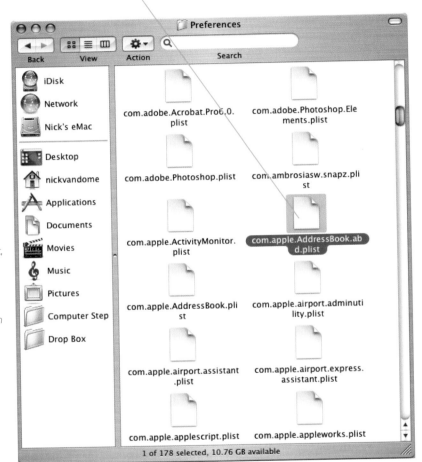

5 Drag the Preferences folder into the Trash. Close the program and then reboot

Problems with programs

The simple answer

OS X is something of a rarity in the world of computing software: it claims to be remarkably stable, and it is. However, this is not to say that things do not sometimes go wrong, although this is considerably less frequent than with older Mac operating systems. Sometimes this will be due to problems within particular programs and on occasions the problems may lie with OS X itself. If this does happen the first course of action is to close down OS X using the Apple menu>Shut Down command. Then restart the computer. If this does not work, or you cannot access the Shut Down command, try turning off the power to the computer and then starting up again.

Force quitting

If a particular program is not responding it can be closed down separately without the need to reboot the computer. To do this:

1 Select Apple menu>Force Quit from the Menu bar

2 Select the program you want to close

3 Click Force Quit

General troubleshooting

It is true that things do go wrong with OS X, although probably with less regularity than with some other operating systems. If something does go wrong, there are a number of items that you can check and also some steps to take to ensure that you do not lose any important data if the worst case scenario occurs and your hard drive packs up completely.

- Back up. If everything does go wrong it is essential to take preventative action in the form of making sure that all of your data is backed up and saved. This can either be done with the Backup program available from the .Mac service or by backing up manually by copying data to a CD or DVD

- Reboot. One traditional reply by IT helpdesks is to reboot i.e. turn off the computer and turn it back on again and hope that the problem has resolved itself. In a lot of cases this simple operation does the trick but it is not always a viable solution for major problems

In extreme cases, you will not be able to reboot your computer normally. If this happens, you will have to pull out the power cable and reattach it. You will then be able to reboot, although the computer may want to check its hard drive to make sure that everything is in working order.

- Check cables. If the problem appears to be with a network connection or an externally connected device, check that all cables are connected properly and have not worked loose. If possible, make sure that all cables are tucked away so that they cannot inadvertently be pulled out

- Check network settings. If your network or Internet connections are not working, check the network setting in System Preferences. Sometimes when you make a change to one item this can have an adverse effect on one of these settings. (If possible, lock the settings once you have applied them, by clicking on the padlock icon in the Network preferences window)

- Check for viruses. If your computer is infected with a virus this could effect the efficient running of the machine. Luckily this is less of a problem for Macs as virus writers tend to concentrate their efforts towards Windows-based machines. However, there are plenty of Mac viruses out there, so make sure your computer is protected by the .Mac virus program, Virex, or a program such as Norton AntiVirus which is available from www.symantec.com

- Check Start-up items. If you have set certain items to start automatically when your computer is turned on, this could cause certain conflicts within your machine. If this is the case, disable the items from launching during the booting up of the computer. This can be done within the Accounts preference of System Preferences by clicking on the Startup Items tab, selecting the relevant item and pressing the minus button

- Check permissions. If you, or other users, are having problems opening items this could be because of the permissions that are set. To check these, select the item in the Finder, click on the Actions button on the Finder toolbar and select Get Info. In the Ownership & Permissions section of the Info window you will be able to set the relevant permissions to allow other users, or yourself, to read, write or have no access

Click here to view permissions settings

- Eject external devices. Sometimes external devices, such as Zip drives, can become temperamental and refuse to eject the disks within them, or even show up on the desktop or in the Finder. If this happens you can eject the disk by pressing the mouse button when the Mac chimes are heard during the booting up process

- Turn-off your screen saver. Screen savers can sometimes cause conflicts within your computer, particularly if they have been downloaded from an unreliable source. If this happens, change the screen saver within the Desktop & Screen Saver preference of the System Preferences or disable it altogether

Restoring software

There may be some instances when you want to restore some of the software that came with OS X, such as if you have deleted a program and then you realize that you require it after all. This can be done with one of the CDs that comes with OS X. However, this does not reinstall OS X itself. To do this you should use the OS X Installation CD and hold down the C key when the Mac chimes are heard. Then follow the installation procedure in the same way as installing the software for the first time. To restore software that came with OS X:

In general you will not have to reinstall OS X unless there is a major problem with your hard drive or a virus has badly affected your system.

1 Double-click on this icon in the Utilities folder

Software Restore

2 Click the Continue button

3 Enter your authentication details (including your user password) and click OK

4 Insert the required disk and follow the on-screen instructions

Index

E

G

F

H

L

M

N

O

P